Hold Fast to Dreams

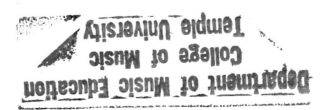

Denise Bacon

Hold Fast
to Dreams

Writings Inspired by
Zoltán Kodály

Kodály Center of America
Wellesley, Massachusetts

Kodály Center of America
15 Denton Road
Wellesley, Massachusetts 02181–9614

Parts of this book appeared in slightly different versions in the
following publications: chapter 1 in Muzsika, December 1972;
chapter 2 in the Dana Hall Bulletin, October–November 1968;
chapter 3 in the International Kodály Society Bulletin, 1983; chapter
10 in the Kodály Center of America Newsletter, June 1992; chapter 19
in the Massachusetts Music Educators News, vol. 32, no. 3 (1984);
and chapter 23 in the International Kodály Society Bulletin, 1977, nos.
1–2.

Printing   5   4   3   2   1

Library of Congress Catalog Card Number 93–77447

ISBN 0–935432–03–5

Printed in the United States of America

Hold fast to dreams, for if dreams die,
Life is a broken-winged bird
that cannot fly.
— Langston Hughes

Dedicated to

Philip DuBois and Helen Land,
whose steadfast support has enabled me
to hold fast to my own dreams

and to

Catherine Filene Shouse,
whose vision, courage, and contribution to
the cultural life of our country
have been a constant source of inspiration.

Foreword

IN THE 1960S AND EARLY 1970S, when music students of my generation were just beginning to come to professional consciousness, there was an atmosphere of excitement and expectancy, particularly among those of us who saw the teaching of music as the ideal way to combine our delight in music with our earnest commitment to social improvement. Nothing exemplified that spirit of hope and change in music education any better than the series of innovations in thinking and practice that appeared in every issue of professional journals. Open classrooms, youth music, creativity, related arts, creative movement, music in early childhood, Suzuki, Dalcroze, Orff, Kodály — so many bandwagons to choose from! Naïveté may not be a wonderful teacher, but it is a wonderful motivator. Workshops on topics like these crowded teachers' weekends, conferences, and summer schedules; "new" was enough of a recommendation. Eventually, the "new" ran out, and after the dust settled, the profession reacted in a number of ways. Some teachers, disappointed, went back to what and how they had been teaching before. The majority, indeed the North American music education profession as a whole, absorbed what seemed to have immediate value from all of these and combined them into as compatible a mixture as possible. A few individuals chose to make an investment of time and resources in one of these concepts to allow it to demonstrate its full effect on music education.

This book is the story of one of these investments. Denise Bacon was a musician and teacher well before anyone in North America had heard of the revolution in music education Zoltán Kodály had inspired in Hungary. When she did come to know of it, however, Denise Bacon made a complete commitment to replicating that revolution here — always with great energy, never without controversy. The collection of Kodály's speeches and writings is called *Visszatekintés* (*Looking Back*). This is Denise Bacon's own "looking ahead" through her articles and speeches. It is a memoir, but not one written from the perspective of hindsight. As we read, we see her perceptions and goals develop and change over the twenty-five years represented. Although the book is a personal account from an individual point of view, it gives valuable insight into the history of the Kodály movement in North America. It reflects her experiences and values, but can help illumine everyone's understanding of the musical, educational, social, and cultural events of the last quarter century.

Bloomington, Indiana, April 1993

Jean Sinor
President,
International Kodály Society

Preface

FOR MANY YEARS, teachers, musical acquaintances, and graduates of the two Kodály institutions associated with my name — the Kodály Musical Training Institute (KMTI) and the Kodály Center of America (KCA) — have urged me to publish a selection of the articles and speeches I have written or delivered over the past twenty-five years. As my editor and I reviewed the more than sixty-five items that have accumulated over that time, we came to realize that they consistently and persistently attempted to communicate the spirit and philosophy of Zoltán Kodály and that they fell into distinct thematic categories. At the same time, many of the well-wishers who have spurred me on to compile this book have also expressed their desire to see a comprehensive history of the Kodály movement in America. Thus a choice was necessary. I decided on the articles and speeches because I think the need is greater and more immediate for an understanding of Kodály's philosophy than for a history of the U.S. development of Kodály's way of music education, and because a history would require extensive, time-consuming research to document the pioneering efforts of others who have made significant contributions to the Kodály cause. In any case, a great deal of history can be gleaned from the content of this book.

The present volume, unfortunately, affords too little space to recount all of the colorful stories and describe all the unforgettable personalities with whom I have worked over the years.* With "a little bit o' luck," the next book will be devoted entirely to those sto-

*In creating an index for this book, I noted with a considerable degree of discomfort that many articles, containing some of the most important names in the development of KMTI, KCA, or the Kodály movement in general, had been eliminated in an effort to avoid duplication of thematic content. I refer to such master teachers as Lenci Igo, Ildiko Herboly, Janos Horvath, Ernö Lendvai, Gábor Ugrin, Éva Sipos, Gabriella Thész, Edith Lantos, Katalin Kiss, and Helga Dietrich; also to such brilliant performers as István Lantos and Boldizsár Keönch. All of these —

ries and those wonderful people — a book that will inevitably be historical, but, I hope, much more interesting than a matter-of-fact chronological history. Leave that to the thesis writers and historians!

I regret that one of the areas of greatest concern to both KMTI and KCA — namely, research on the effects of Kodály-based education — has had to be excluded from this collection in the interest of brevity. It is ironic that, had it not been for Dr. Charles Drake,† who persistently encouraged but also needled me to get down to business, to stop procrastinating, and to actually produce what I'd been talking about for years, this book would still be only a figment of my imagination. It is ironic, because Dr. Drake made possible two of the research projects that resulted in significant funding for both KMTI and KCA. Scientifically designed Kodály-based research deserves serious consideration but has received scant attention, and it is my hope that some of the thoughts expressed in these writings will stimulate interest in such research.

This volume is arranged into five parts, each touching on the efforts I and others have made to adapt the Kodály concept to American culture. Part One represents a combined historical-philosophical approach covering my meetings with Zoltán Kodály in the 1960s, my subsequent studies in Hungary, and my efforts to establish quality teacher training based on authentic Kodály principles in the United States.

In Part Two of this book, I have brought together various writings that attempt to shed light on and interpret Kodály's philosophy.

Part Three addresses the way Kodály educators may use that philosophy to combat some of the pernicious effects of modern society, to counteract the erosion of basic human values that is evident to all of us.

Part Four presents controversies and problems surrounding the Kodály concept — the controversies being either ideological

---

and surely there are others — significantly influenced the directions I took and contributed immeasurably to the quality standard for which the leading U.S. Kodály programs are known today. They deserve to be recognized.

†Dr. Charles Drake, a leading pioneer in the field of dyslexia, is a former chairman of the KCA Board of Trustees and current board member.

(musically) or connected to my position on goals, objectives, and the future direction of the Kodály movement in America. These writings also address the problems dealing with adaptation of the Kodály concept to specific situations such as the inner city and foreign cultures.

Part Five asks just who a Kodály teacher is, and what sort of training produces that special person.

I would like to explain how footnotes and source notes have been handled. The footnotes in some cases are an important illumination of the text; in other cases, they are parts of articles not included in this book that have special relevance to the article to which they are attached and that I really did not want to leave out. Such footnotes are identified by symbols (asterisks and so forth). Numbered source notes identifying quotations are placed at the end of each chapter so as not to interrupt the flow of the text.

Within each part, the writings are arranged chronologically, in order to present changes in my thinking over the years. Consequently, to move from the end of one part to the beginning of the next can mean jumping back two decades or more. Please be patient with these jumps in time and context as you read the book, and please also take into account the year the article or speech was written and the changes that have occurred since. You may note a certain amount of outdated terminology in the earliest articles, such as "ghetto," the use of "he" for a person of unspecified gender, etc. Since these were the terms in use when the articles were written, I have left them as in the original. As such terminology became an issue, however, I adjusted accordingly. Otherwise, I have noted major changes in my own thinking, such as my repudiation of the word *method*, as they occurred, through the use of footnotes where necessary.

Many of the speeches were originally written for the opening or closing exercises of KMTI or KCA summer and academic-year courses. They were personally addressed to our students and faculty and generally reflected my goals for American music education. The goals I have had — raising the standard of teacher training; dignifying the role of music educators; closing the gap between music educators and performers; educating teachers, parents, and publishers about the necessity of identifying, using, and making available materials of lasting value, based on cultural heritage — have been only partially realized and will be achieved only through a continuing concerted effort on the part of many committed people.

My basic goals have not changed over the past twenty-five years. Finding the way to achieve them requires imagination, vision, and flexibility, along with recognition and acceptance of constantly changing educational theories, policies, and social conditions. If the Kodály concept is to survive, it must either choose to play the role of preserving the best of its European-based, Western, classical tradition in music, or it must seek and find the way to adapt its basic tenets to changing demographic patterns. To survive *and* be successful means going both routes. The wonderful wealth of Western musical tradition must somehow be preserved, lest it be obliterated and drown in the rising tide of varying cultures seeking assimilation into the global community. On the other hand, we are the losers if we do not learn to understand and appreciate the music of other cultures. For music, in my opinion, should not be exclusively an end in itself; it is also, perhaps more importantly, a vehicle for communication and understanding. It is exciting to imagine that, just possibly, the Kodály philosophy might be one thread that can bind us together and help us find the way to a common understanding of each other's needs, hopes, and dreams.

I believe that these articles and speeches, though written over a period of twenty-five years, are still relevant. They record the basic truth that nothing ever stays the same — that "the only constant is change." Much has changed since Kodály's ideas first came to our shores, and there must be further change before his visionary plans can be translated to practical reality. Above all, I hope that these writings will forever dispel the notion that Kodály's "method" is the important thing; rather, it is his thought, spirit, and philosophy that can inspire our present activities and point a way to a better future for music education.

Wellesley, Massachusetts, April 1993   Denise Bacon

Acknowledgments

MANY PEOPLE have advised me about the content of this book and helped in its preparation.

First of all, the book would never have materialized had it not been for Estelle Kaczenas's insistence of keeping a meticulous record of every speech and article I ever wrote, and for Valerie Von Rosenvinge, who finally collected the materials chronologically into readable form so that they could be selected and edited.

I am grateful to Péter and Ida Erdei, Betsy Moll, and Jean Sinor for encouraging me to produce writings of a philosophical nature, rather than a chronological history, and for advice and help with many details.

I am indebted to the following:

to my colleagues Faith Knowles and Ingrid Kainen, who between them read all of the original articles and made invaluable suggestions concerning their inclusion, omission, or adaptation.

to Diane Weiseman for taking care of the myriad frustrating details that kept cropping up.

to Sarolta Kodály for help in choosing the best photographs, and for advice concerning copyright and permissions.

to Andrea Jávor and Gábor Bognár of MTI Interfoto, Budapest, for providing the cover picture of Zoltán Kodály.

to David Giele, my good friend and neighbor, former managing editor of the College Division at Little, Brown and Co., for advice on how to proceed with publishers, editors, and those responsible for the production of the book.

to Jayne Moore, who expertly retyped many articles and incorporated corrections made in my often unreadable handwriting.

to Vivian Klein for help with the index.

to Gábor Viragh for help with accents on Hungarian names!

to Wayne Ellis, who so ably took on all aspects of the book's design and production and was unfailingly patient and understanding about my questions and many changes.

to Alison Scott for her tasteful cover design.

to Corey Field of European American Publishers for advice about publishing and help with marketing.

Two persons whose opinion I have always valued highly, and whose suggestions I knew I could rely upon, read the book in its formative stages and provided valuable insight:

Estelle Kaczenas, KCA's Administrative Director (now retired) who supported me in whatever task I undertook but who also never failed to tell me where to get off when she felt I was wrong.

Helen Bryan, friend, visionary, and innovator, whose extraordinary efforts to make the Kodály concept available to a wider public have significantly advanced the cause of the Kodály movement.

I am grateful to two persons who agreed to read the finished manuscript and to give an objective assessment of its concept from varying perspectives:

to Betty Allen, noted mezzo-soprano and Director, The Harlem School of the Arts.

to Barbara Kaplan, Professor Emerita, Auburn University, and former editor of the *Kodály Envoy*, who also made valuable editorial suggestions.

My thanks also to:

Jean Sinor, Director of Undergraduate Studies, Indiana University School of Music, and President of the International Kodály Society, for taking time from her almost inhuman schedule of commitments to write a Foreword.

László Eösze, musicologist, author, and former Artistic Director of Editio Musica, Budapest, 1961–1987, for his beautiful Appreciation and for help with photos and important corrections.

I also wish to thank KCA's Board of Trustees for their forbearance and encouragement throughout this time-consuming project. I never knew just how much was involved in producing such a book!

However, the lion's share of the credit belongs to my editor, Larry Hamberlin, whose long experience in both publishing and music and whose infallible sense of the rightness and wrongness of things saved me from almost certain disaster—such as trying to publish all sixty-five of my articles and speeches in one book! I can now safely predict that no one would ever have read the book had he not found a way, through clever organization of the articles around specific themes, eliminating repetition, and adding footnotes, to condense the most important parts of those sixty-five essays into the book's present form.

Lastly, I owe a large debt to those teachers and colleagues, both American and Hungarian, who are too many to acknowledge individually, but whose labor in behalf of Kodály's philosophy over the years has continuously inspired my efforts.

Wellesley, Massachusetts, April 1993   Denise Bacon

This book was made possible in part by a generous contribution from the Seth Sprague Educational and Charitable Foundation of New York.

Denise Bacon: An Appreciation

AFTER THE MOSAIC-LIKE RICHNESS of 44 short reviews of distinguished personalities from all over the world (*Reflections on Kodály*, L. Vikár, 1985, and *The Legacy of Zoltán Kodály*, M. A. Hein, 1992), Denise Bacon has now presented us with a thorough outline of the developing history of the American Kodály movement from 1968 to 1982.

While she is telling us her own story, we become aware at every turn that her activity and the American Kodály movement are interdependent.

It was she, the bright-minded artist, who discovered what that small and poor European country, Hungary, can offer to a wealthy and mighty continent like America.

It was she, a complete musician, who transplanted the benefits of Kodály's philosophy and spirit to her native country.

It was she, the enthusiastic teacher, who, inspired by Kodály, became strong enough to inspire young educators to continuously improve their work, strengthening the very humanity in a computer-dominated, pushbutton society.

The papers and lectures she has compiled in this volume afford good reading and are most convincing. Her authenticity is beyond dispute, the fountainhead of her knowledge being the lifework of Kodály, which she has seriously investigated.

Denise Bacon, touched once by the magic accomplished by Kodály's educational concept, started her uncompromising struggle for raising the level of American musical life in 1965. Insisting always on quality, she has continued working through nearly three decades. Her activity is an example for all those who are striving for the spiritual growth of young people.

Kodály once said, "It is our firm conviction that mankind will live the happier when it has learned to live with music more worthily.

Whoever works to promote this end in one way or another, has not lived in vain."

Denise Bacon is such a person.

Budapest, April 1993   László Eösze

Artistic Director,
Editio Musica, Budapest,
1961–1987

Contents

PART THREE
Kodály and Human Values

PART FOUR
Controversies Surrounding the Kodály Concept

PART FIVE
The Kodály-Trained Teacher: "Trained Ears, Mind, Heart, and Hands"

Illustration sections begin on pages 68, 93, 131, and 184

Prologue: "Hold Fast to Dreams"

This prologue is adapted from the graduation address of the Kodály Center of America's 1982 summer course at Southeastern Massachusetts University.

"Hold fast to dreams, for if dreams die, life is but a broken-winged bird that cannot fly." This quotation from Langston Hughes is taped on the pantry door that leads to my garage, so that I can neither leave my house every morning nor go into the dining room without seeing it. If I can give you nothing else in this book, I can give you this quotation; it will help to sustain you for a lifetime. Below this quotation on my pantry door is another, by Flo Lund's daughter, who was thirteen years old when Flo brought it to me one day. It says: "A negative thinker is a positive stinker."

These two quotations have helped me through the past twenty-three years, reminding me that no matter how difficult or disastrous the events of any given day may appear to be, nothing in truth can possibly have occurred that, as Og Mandino says, "will not seem insignificant in the river of centuries," [1] and that it is only my own reaction to difficulties that will prevent me from solving them.

Our world is in such a condition now that it is difficult to hold fast to dreams and difficult not to be negative. It is much easier to cave in to despair, and it is often a great temptation to do so. The more mechanized we become, the more our computer existence appears to take over the direction of our lives, the closer our technological progress forces groups of seemingly unrelated people from distant parts of the globe to be aware of each other, then the greater the confusion and the greater our feeling of individual helplessness to shape our own personal destinies. We can too easily become lost in the shuffle, feel inadequate to cope, useless or powerless to effect change; we feel like insignificant snowflakes gathered up and absorbed beyond recognition in the snowballing tempo of life.

The greatest problem of our times is not economic or personal security, but rather communication — how to get along with one another in our families, our jobs, our communities, our domestic politics, our public relations and foreign policies around the world. It is just as difficult (if not more so) for Hungarians, Mexicans, Canadians, Australians, South Africans, or Middle Easterners as for Americans to live in today's world. But the Kodály movement has been a beautiful example of intercultural communication. It has been successful because we share common goals and ideals. It is why, no matter how proficient Americans may become as teachers, or how able to disseminate Kodály's philosophy to others, it has been important not to hold courses without our Hungarian colleagues, and to accept foreign students with open arms. They have enabled us to reevaluate our own country's strengths and weaknesses and to recognize the privileges and opportunities we too often take for granted.

Those who have had authentic Kodály training know that it is more than a musical learning experience — it is a preparation for living. They have learned that a philosophy of teaching or living cannot be acquired overnight and adapted from one culture to another through the gimmicks or teaching tools that are sometimes mistakenly labeled "the Kodály method."

Because there are far too few places where one can receive in-depth, sound Kodály training, either here or abroad, we must encourage and commend all those who are willing to commit their energies to training and to establishing Kodály-based programs. The strong programs leading to certificate or diploma can be counted on the fingers of one hand and are far apart geographically. Nonetheless, I have been amazed and gratified at the international development that has taken place since 1970, when twenty-six Americans from the first Kodály summer course at the 1969 Dana School of Music attended the first Kodály summer seminar in Kecskemét, Hungary. Twelve years later, in 1982, when I spoke about the early development of the American adaptation at the Tenth International Seminar in Kecskemét, there were 120 foreigners from twenty-four countries and five continents — from Russia to South America; from Australia to Africa; from Japan to Czechoslovakia. My speech recounting the early steps of adaptation in America was received with tremendous enthusiasm; many wanted to know more about how to start or develop the Kodály concept further in their respective countries. Students from the Kodály Center of America who attended the seminar felt somewhat overwhelmed and said they had not realized what had gone into the development of the Kodály concept in the United States. This book, I hope, will tell part of that story. The important thing at the time, however, was not the speech but the reaction and result. The group of American students from KCA, KMTI, and Indiana University sang the song *We Gather Here Together* (*Harmonia Mundi* in Canada), which by 1982 had become a sort of theme song of the North American Kodály movement. The participants of the other countries were thrilled with that song, and when I translated it for the Hungarians, and the Russian, Polish, Japanese, and French simultaneous translators did the same for their respective groups, there were tears in the eyes of many. It is a lovely thought that we can sing that song and share common goals together across an ocean and half a world away.

There in Kecskemét in 1982 I could feel the miracle of togetherness with those 190 people, as I have felt it ever since at meetings of the Organization of American Kodály Educators (OAKE), at the International Kodály Society meetings in Athens and Calgary, and wherever I have attended Kodály gatherings in the United States or elsewhere. And I believe strongly that the time is coming when, as Kodály envisioned, "all people in all lands are brought together through singing, and when there is a universal harmony." It is beginning to happen, and it is a truly wonderful experience to feel it in foreign groups representing so many cultures.

Music is a priceless gift that can never be taken away from you;

you will never lose it if you make a point of including it in your daily life. Guard it carefully, as it is more precious than you may imagine, when real trouble strikes.

One day at the last KCA summer course in which she taught, Kati Komlós* brought me a card for no particular reason except that she thought I would like it. It contained a quotation by Christian D. Larson with which I would like to close this prologue:

> Promise yourself to be so strong that nothing can disturb your peace of mind. To talk health, happiness and prosperity to every person you meet. To make all your friends feel that there is something in them. To look at the sunny side of everything and make your optimism come true. To think only of the best, to work only for the best and expect only the best. To be just as enthusiastic about the success of others as you are about your own. To forget the mistakes of the past and press on to the greater achievements of the future. To wear a cheerful countenance at all times and give every living creature you meet a smile. To give so much time to the improvement of yourself that you have no time to criticize others. To be too large for worry, too noble for anger, too strong for fear and too happy to permit the presence of trouble.

To promise oneself anything, one must first imagine and dream. And so I wish for you who read this book only the most beautiful dreams, the courage to hold fast to them, and the strength and determination to make them come true.

[1] Og Mandino, *The Greatest Salesman in the World* (New York: Frederick Fell, 1968).

*At the time KMTI was founded, Mrs. Kodály recommended that Denise Bacon invite Katalin Komlós, then a researcher at the Institute of Musicology of the Hungarian Academy of Sciences in Budapest, to help find the material needed to build an American Kodály-based curriculum. Kati Komlós spent three academic years at KMTI, from 1970 to 1972, researching American folk material; she was coeditor, with Péter Erdei, of *150 American Folk Songs to Sing, Read and Play* (Boosey and Hawkes, 1974). A fine pianist, she also performed in and directed summer course chamber music activities, and taught solfege at both KMTI and KCA for a period of more than fifteen years.

[4]

Part One

Developing the
Kodály Concept
in the United States:
A Personal Account

1. Kodály's Legacy to America

This chapter first appeared in Hungarian in the Kodály Memorial Issue of Muzsika, December 1972, in a translation by Péter Erdei.

Although I met Zoltán Kodály on a few occasions and even asked several questions of him personally, I could never say I knew him. Yet to be in his presence, even briefly, was an experience of lasting impact. One could not remain unchanged under the scrutiny of his steady, penetrating gaze. It was as if a powerful beam of light suddenly struck and exposed my innermost being for what it really was. One moment of his direct glance was enough to make me wonder what I had ever done with my life that could be considered worthwhile. The result of my brief encounter with him was a certainty that whatever I had done before was not enough.

I first met Kodály in July 1965 at Dartmouth College, in Hanover, New Hampshire, where he was composer-in-residence at Dartmouth's Summer Congregation of the Arts. There, over an unhurried cup of tea with his beautiful young wife, Sarolta, in the spacious home made available for his visit, we talked about the problems of American music education — the poor taste of the public, the eroding effects of television, the diminishing audience for good music and dwindling attendance at live concerts, the terrible diet of composed trash given our children in the public schools, the lamentably poor training of music teachers in most colleges and conservatories.

His reactions to my complaints and answers to

my questions shattered my complacency and made me realize how useless were my good intentions, if not followed up by action. In one moment I realized he knew more about what was *really* going on in American music education than I, an American, did. Speaking from a sheltered position as the director of a small private community music school,* with the background of a performing artist (I was a pianist), I had observed the results of general American music education without understanding the reasons underlying our deteriorating situation.

Kodály's first advice to me was to join the Music Educators National Conference (MENC), the largest organized group of music educators in the United States, numbering at that time over seventy thousand members. This I did, and at the same time I began to investigate musical and educational conditions in various parts of the country. By the following summer of 1966, when I again met Kodály at Stanford University, I was even more distressed at the magnitude of the problem confronting serious music educators who wanted a change.

After listening to inspired lectures by both Kodály and Professor Erzsébet Szönyi of the Liszt Academy telling of Kodály's efforts to change conditions in Hungary over the previous fifty years, I asked how we could do the same in America, especially when we were a mixture of so many cultures. Kodály replied that *because* our country was so much bigger and represented so many nationalities, we had the richest melting pot of folk culture in the world. He thus turned what seemed to be a big obstacle into a major asset.

The next summer at the International Society of Music Educators (ISME) 1966 conference at Interlochen, Michigan, I had an opportunity to see the truth of one of Kodály's strongest beliefs — that music is an international language, capable of bringing the peoples of the world together in closer harmony. There I also had the opportunity to meet the other Hungarian music teachers who were

---

*At that time I was the head of the music department of a trilogy of private girls' schools (Tenacre, Dana Hall, and Pine Manor) and the director of the Dana School of Music, all in Wellesley, Massachusetts.

to become key figures in my decision to attempt the establishment of a Kodály Institute in the United States: Márta Nemesszeghy, Katalin Forrai, Helga Szabó, and Klára Kokas. Their enthusiasm, knowledge, broad vision, and commitment to Kodály's ideas inspired me to want to come to Hungary to find out for myself what was going on there in music educational circles. Both Kodály and Erzsébet Szönyi said they would help me if I would come. As I said goodbye to Kodály at the end of the conference, I explained that I had no money but that, somehow, I would find a way to come the next summer to Hungary. I will never forget his comment — he said, almost prophetically, "If there is a next summer." I thought it very strange, as he was so strong, so healthy, so active in that summer of 1966.

I subsequently applied for and was fortunate to receive a grant from the Braitmayer Foundation, supplemented by a grant from the Dana Hall trustees,† which allowed me to spend a whole academic year in Europe. I looked forward so much to going, to receiving Kodály's advice and help. But I was never to meet Kodály again. When I received the news of his death in March 1967, I was stunned and dismayed. All my friends asked me, "Will you go to Hungary now that Kodály is gone?" I replied that of course I would, that the fruits of his lifelong labor were as important as the man himself and that from them I could learn — only it would be more difficult without his guiding hand.

Kodály always said Americans intended well, but wanted everything immediately — overnight, and given to them on a silver platter. He said we did everything too fast. Well, I am afraid I was one of those, too. Even in my own country, I had not been accustomed to dealing with government authorities and was not aware of the way all governments operate — whether in the East or West — that there is a certain amount of red tape one must necessarily cut

†The Braitmayer Foundation awarded grants to teachers for innovative projects in various disciplines through the National Association of Independent Schools (NAIS), of which Dana Hall was a member institution. Had it not been for these two grants, I might never have traveled to Hungary or followed the path in which that decisive year of study (1967–68) led me.

through. Looking back on what has been accomplished since the year I spent in Hungary, I am increasingly amazed, appreciative, and grateful for the fast and courteous treatment I received from Hungarian authorities everywhere — in the Hungarian Ministry of Education, at the Liszt Academy, in the Kecskemét Town and County Council. These organizations and many others, such as Kultint, Interkoncert, Kultura, and Zenemükiadó, have contributed to the realization of my dream that we could establish an institute in the United States that would have a direct, live connection to present Hungarian musical life.

It is important for all Hungarians to realize the legacy that Kodály has left, not only to Hungary but to the whole world. The fruits of his lifework can be seen on the faces of children singing in the school choirs of Hungary. These children, for the most part (at least wherever the instruction is good), take pleasure in the music itself. They join choirs, not mainly for the social opportunities they present, but for the love of performing good music. Young children and young adults of this generation enjoy a fine concert — furthermore, they go to hear the music, not only for the performer. I was often surprised in Hungary by how many fine performers appeared on the same program and by how many artists shared the spotlight, that there was not usually an individual "star." How much more interesting for the audience, how much richer the experience, how much deeper the learning when one can be exposed to a variety of periods and styles and can make comparisons between artists' interpretations!

In our country this kind of concertgoing and love of music is rare, because we have been brought up on the star system. Many a gifted young instrumentalist practices eight hours a day for many long years, not for the joy of the music, but so he may reach the top of the heap, so he may have star billing, so he need *not* share the program with others. The sad thing is that when he has reached that lofty pinnacle, there is often no one to hear him. The same is true of composers. So few of our young composers are willing to use their talent for children as Kodály did. They prefer to write two measures a week or three pages a year; they struggle endlessly to be different — to write works of such individuality that they will gain immortality and be remembered down the ages. But who is there to hear them?

The audience of yesterday was an elite one, in all countries of the world. Only those possessing "culture" (at that time usually synonymous with money) were able to "appreciate" fine art, drama, and music. The Socialist countries have changed all that so that the road to culture may be traveled by everyone. Even in the United States there is broad opportunity for education, in spite of our terrible imbalances and extremes of poverty and wealth. The average person can afford culture, but sadly enough, does not want it. Kodály brought about a renaissance of culture based on true Hungarian roots. He proved that one does not have to be high-born, wealthy, or talented to be touched by great art. His constant demand that only the best in music, literature, and art be given to children has paid rich dividends. It is no mere accident or difference in basic cultures that a Hungarian child, when asked what he wants for his birthday or for a present, often answers that he wants a book, where an American child will usually ask for a toy, which can be destroyed overnight. Everywhere in America one sees evidence of what Kodály so often complained about — "that to expose a child to something which is in poor taste when he is young will poison his soul for life."

Kodály's gift to Hungary and to the world will be fully understood only in years to come. That gift is great because the thought behind it was great. He believed in the dignity and worth of the individual human being and wanted every person to reach his own potential. This goal could be achieved only through excellence and high demands placed on the individual in every walk and category of life, whether student, teacher, scholar, or worker.

We have many musical problems in both our countries and many other pressing problems, too. But the guiding hand of Kodály can be felt everywhere in the spirit and lifework of those he left behind. It is our task to try to prove the truth of his conviction that "mankind will live the happier when it has learned to live with music more worthily." [1]

[1] Zoltán Kodály, *Selected Writings* (Budapest: Corvina Press, 1974), p. 206.

2. A Year Behind the Iron Curtain

This chapter first appeared in the Dana Hall Bulletin, October–November 1968.

Had anyone gazed into a crystal ball in June 1966 and predicted that two years later I would have spent a whole academic year in Budapest, Hungary, I would have reacted with utter astonishment and disbelief. Yet that is what happened.

Following my meetings with Kodály at Stanford University and Interlochen and a six-month struggle to obtain a visa, I arrived in Budapest on October 2, 1967. Excited though I was at the prospect of a new adventure, my first impressions as I drove through the city to the Hotel Astoria were of shocked disbelief — everywhere were bullet-pierced buildings, streets torn up, very old cars and taxis, hordes of people, and dirt, dirt, dirt. I had never been to Europe or any war-ravaged country before, and I asked the driver if the bullet holes and damaged buildings were from the 1956 revolution or the 1945 war. He answered blithely that there were no evidences of past war, that this had all been cleaned up. I decided I had better keep quiet and not ask provocative questions until I knew my way around a little better.

The Astoria Hotel was a busy tourist hotel that reflected a bygone era of genteel nineteenth-century elegance. My room was pleasant enough, and I was charmed by the old-fashioned courtesy of the chambermaids — they were incredulous and unbelievably pleased when I offered a tip for drawing a bath or bringing my breakfast. But I had not anticipated either the communications problem or the monstrous head cold that assailed me the night I arrived.

The next morning I was whisked off to the Ministry of Education for a briefing and a request for two hundred dollars for the first month's tuition, which, it was explained, was for the "course" I would take. Since I had no intention of being straitjacketed into any prearranged "course," I'm afraid I presented a not-too-favorable first impression to the Hungarian authorities, especially in view of my bulbous red nose, nasal voice, and puffy eyes. In spite of this, they were very kind to me and celebrated my arrival quite formally with brandy (at 10 A.M.) and speeches.

Later in that first day, I took a taxi to Erzsébet Szönyi's house. Prof. Szönyi has taken over Kodály's mantle since his death and is responsible for spreading his method internationally. Dean of the music education faculty at the Liszt Academy, she is one of Hungary's leading composers and the only present link for spreading Kodály's ideas to the Western world. She immediately made all possible arrangements, opened many doors, and offered her warm personal friendship.

The small living room in which she received me was crammed with pictures of Kodály and other famous people, testimonials, and books on music in many languages, four of which she speaks fluently. It was pouring rain when I arrived, the house was chilly with no heat, and as we sat sipping brandy in the gathering darkness (no lights were put on until it was totally dark), I reflected on the way of life of this already well known, successful woman.

Her home had been a modest but comfortable one in a very good neighborhood, with a nice garden. Hungary, like many of the other small European nations, had always been a feudal state, with a small ruling minority controlling all the wealth. Moreover, for thousands of years Hungarians had been dominated in turn by Romans, Turks, Austrians, Germans, and most recently, Russians. The ruling minority during World War II believed it could best protect its interests by joining the Nazis, much to the distress of ninety-five percent of the Hungarian people, who had wanted to join the Allies. Prof. Szönyi's house, like many others in Budapest, was first used by Hungarian army officers, then German, and finally Russian. She told me that she and her family lived for two months with thirty other people in a cellar a few blocks away, without heat, light, or other conveniences. The living room I sat in had been used to keep officers' horses out of the winter cold.

When the Russians "liberated" Budapest in 1945, most of the population was overjoyed because the Nazis were driven out. Prof. Szönyi's house was then divided into four apartments; she, her husband (a lawyer), and two sons now occupied three rooms, a kitchen, hallway, and bath. Prof. Szönyi was fortunate in that her mother and mother-in-law were able to share one of the other apartments. This talented woman earns one of the highest salaries in Budapest (exclusive, of course, of party political positions, which pay very well by Hungary's economic standard) — about five thousand dollars a year. Most teachers earn from forty to seventy dollars a month.

When I left, I asked Prof. Szönyi to call me a taxi. She was shocked that I would take one and explained that her house was only five minutes' walk to a bus that would take me back into town (she lived in a hilly section of Buda, about thirty minutes from the center of Pest). I quickly discovered I would be branded either a rich American capitalist or a party member if I took taxis to get places.

The transportation problem was one of the most annoying aspects of life in Budapest — streetcars and buses were always jammed, I repeatedly lost buttons off my coats, and my shoes were worn out before Christmas from being continuously stepped on. In addition, one often had to wait while several buses went by, as it was impossible to get on; it was rarely possible to get a taxi in such a situation, however — especially if it was raining, or cold, or rush hour. There were only six hundred taxis in this city of over two million people. I was afraid I would be unable to make my 9 A.M. plane to Boston the morning of July 29, 1968, when I was to leave Budapest for good, as I could not even order a taxi at 11 P.M. the night before — the taxi stands simply will not answer to take calls for the next day if they are busy at the moment. (At 2 A.M. I was finally successful in ordering a cab for seven the next morning.)

Almost no one owns a car except party members. Therefore I made it a point not to ride in a car. Volkswagens are most prominent of the available makes but cost about $4,500 — an unthinkable sum for most Hungarians. One never sees gas stations — I can think of only two in Budapest. I almost never rode in a car, however. Perhaps there were more.

The telephone situation was a real nightmare. I stayed in the Hotel Astoria for ten days while I hunted for an appropriate room. I had been there less than a week when I had the good fortune to sell a Cape Cod house that I owned and had been trying to sell for four years. Telegrams are almost as bad as telephones, and one must use the telephone to send a telegram if one does not want to spend two to three hours at a post office (the more usual way to send a telegram). After several unsuccessful attempts to communicate with my lawyer by telegram, and after several crossed wires, he sent me a telegram instructing me to phone him. The operators in the Astoria, with whom I always had to speak a gibberish of German, French, English, and Hungarian in order to make myself understood, could not believe I would telephone the United States, especially at twelve dollars a minute. Neither did I! I did so three times during the year, however, and each time nearly suffered a nervous collapse. I became famous all over the hotel — porters, elevator men, chambermaids, and dining room waiters could not do enough for me. I think they thought I was the richest American in the world. I even began to think so myself from the way I was being treated.

When I moved to my rented room, my landlady was good enough to allow me to use the phone. I could rarely make it work, however — sometimes nothing happened at all, the line went completely dead for no apparent reason; or it would ring and ring incessantly in a big institution like the Ministry of Education, the Liszt Academy, or a railroad station, where someone was certain to be, but no one would answer; or else someone would answer and quickly hang up because he could not understand my Hungarian; or someone would take it off the hook but say nothing, and after waiting five minutes, I would be cut off. In any case, though one tried three days ahead to make an appointment to see a particular person, there was absolutely no guarantee one would be able to reach that person in three days' time. The only way to be certain

closed for inventory, or moved to another location; the manager was on vacation or would be back in an hour; they had butter yesterday but not today; or they sold fruit last week but only vegetables this week.

The word best used to describe living conditions in Budapest is *frustration* — no matter what one tried to do, one couldn't do it. Yet I would not have traded this experience for anything in the world. I cried when I left. I have left a part of my heart there and I cannot wait to go back.

Why? Because the people I met were a freedom-loving people, living under foreign domination, struggling with their tragic situation in a most heroic and selfless way. They took me in with unquestioning trust and opened their hearts and homes to me. Though they had little, they would have given me their last cent. They shared everything. They accepted my being an American, even though they neither understood why the United States did not help them in 1956 nor why we were currently involved in Vietnam. The news, which I watched regularly on my landlady's television set (which had only one channel) was naturally presented along party lines in the light of Communist philosophy. Yet Hungarians know that fundamentally Americans are not evil, that they are free and also prosperous. Therefore, they want to like us. I love the Hungarians because they are talented people — their folk music and their three great composers, Liszt, Bartók, and Kodály, have left the world a priceless musical heritage. I love them because they are a people seemingly born to tragedy who yet laugh and are gay. Their sense of values is real; that is, value has to do with the fundamental aspects of life. They are more concerned with nonmaterial values, perhaps because they have had to be. A stroll on the Margaret Island to see the peacocks, the gardens, and the colored fountains give the average person as much pleasure as a Broadway musical would give an American. Teenagers do not give flowers to dates or spend money on them otherwise; a window-shopping expedition or a trip to the park with a stop at an espresso stand for coffee and a tart is enough for an evening's entertainment.

This brings me to a concept I would never have accepted before spending this year behind the Iron Curtain: I can no longer believe that all communism is totally evil. After seeing the results it has achieved for a large segment of the permanently deprived population, such as enough food, clothing, inexpensive entertainment of high artistic standard, and an education for every man, woman, and child, I can no longer question the benefits of its proven achievements. I rather question whether the means justify the ends and whether this particular brand of Soviet communism is worth such results. The Hungarian people have paid a terrible price for the advances made — they have paid with their personal freedom. Even the most violent Hungarian anti-Communist (less than ten percent are registered party members) will tell you that life is better now for the great mass of people than it was prior to the Communists' coming in 1945. But nearly all of them hate the imposed Russian domination, both politically and culturally. What they do want and believe in is another kind of communism, the type of democratic socialism that Czechoslovakia had been struggling so hard to achieve before the tragic invasion.

In my short trips through other parts of Europe during the year, I was shocked and distressed to see large banners in Italy and France saying, "Vote Communist." I thought, "How could they? They can't possibly know what it is really like and how lucky they are." But I later came to realize that France and Italy were advocating and demanding a different kind of communism — as different from Soviet communism as night is from day. It is hard for the average American to realize that Europe's problems probably cannot be solved in the same way America's have been. In the first place, though we have slums and unemployment, we do not have a population of which seventy percent is living in abject poverty, without even the fundamental necessities of life. Since it has never been true in history that the small ruling minorities in feudal states have been willing to share, and is not true today that the haves are voluntarily going to give to the have-nots, it is reasonable to assume that a type of communism that provides for the wants of the seventy percent is going to gain support whether Americans like it or not.

The average American associates all communism with Soviet

communism. Yet when I went to Prague last May, I was immediately struck by differences in both the living conditions and attitudes of the Czech people compared to what I had found in Hungary and East Berlin. The people of Prague were proud, their stores were full, American capital was pouring money into new hotels, and the attitude was defiant, fiercely independent, and disdainful of anything Soviet. They wanted communism, but they wanted their own kind, which I could see imitated many facets of Western life and thought and which would certainly have been a bridge between Soviet communism and Western capitalism.

I had intended to write about my musical experiences in both Hungary and other parts of Europe. Though I went to Europe for musical reasons, and cannot underestimate the value of what I learned there, musically speaking, I find it has been the social and political aspects of my year there that have impressed me most and probably will remain with me permanently.

One cannot write about such an experience without touching on education. One of the greatest differences between the Eastern and Western concepts of education is the light in which the individual evaluates his education. In Hungary, the young high school or university student values education for two reasons: first, for what it will give him for himself in later years and for the personal pleasure he will derive from knowledge; second, as a possible means of getting out to the Western world. He does not view education from the point of view of economic necessity, as we do in this country.

One of the fruits of an Eastern education is an ability to discriminate, to judge what is valuable. Though Hungarians are poor and desperately need money, they do not value it as highly as less material possessions. They would much prefer to spend their time doing something that they like to do than in acquiring money. They cannot understand why so many of our decisions are based on financial considerations. They are more interested in permanent, though less tangible properties, which cannot be taken away from them. They have so little material wealth that very small pleasures mean a great deal — excursions to the mountains, visits to friends. But education is also valued as an escape to another realm. The average city dweller goes frequently to opera, theater, and concert, all of which are very cheap. If I ask a child, "Which do you like better — the music you learn in school, or rock 'n' roll and the Beatles?" he will answer me, "The music we learn in school is great art and is therefore always valuable; the other music is part of our social life and we like it. They are not the same, and we do not wish to do without either one."

The Kodály method is so much more than a musical method — it is a total educational philosophy. It is far in advance of anything we are doing in this country in music education, and I am vitally interested in transplanting as much of it as can be successfully adapted here.

3. Adapting the Kodály Concept in America, 1965–1982

This chapter is adapted from a paper delivered at the Tenth International Kodály Seminar, Zoltán Kodály Pedagogical Institute of Music, Kecskemét, Hungary, July 1982. The paper was published in an abridged version as "The Adaptation of Kodály's Concept of Music Education in America: Early Steps — An Historical Perspective" in the International Kodály Society Bulletin, 1983.

The story begins in the mid-1960s. A music teacher from California, Mary Helen Richards, while traveling in Europe with her family, visited some schools in Budapest and was astonished by the children's singing. She met Zoltán Kodály, who gave her a copy of the first-grade children's book for the twice weekly (as opposed to the daily singing school) music classes,* originally written at Kodály's request by the brilliant pedagogue Jenö Ádám. Upon her return to the United States, she wrote a book of her own, Threshold to Music, modeled on Ádám's book and supplemented with large pictorial charts. This book, presented at several one- and two-day workshops by Mrs. Richards, was an immediate success.† American teachers had never

*"[Musical] literacy is achieved under two different systems; the rate of progress depends on whether a child is in a school that has music twice a week or in one that has it every day. If only twice a week, the child can read music in sol-fa by second grade, but not in letter names, so that it may be applied to an instrument, until fourth or fifth grade. Those who have music every day can read and write music with letter names by second grade" ("Kodály and Orff: Report from Europe," Music Educators Journal, April 1969).

†Mary Helen Richards also developed a model school in Palo Alto, California. "In Mrs. Richards's early efforts, she was joined by Katinka Daniel, who had received her training at the Liszt Academy in Budapest as a piano major." Katinka Daniel later "branched off from Mary Helen Richards ... and established one of the first models at the San Roque Parochial School in Santa Barbara, California" ("The Kodály Concept in the U.S.," Hungarian Quarterly, Autumn 1976).

seen or heard anything like it. Furthermore, it appeared to be so clear, so logical and easy, that even regular classroom teachers, non-musicians, could teach from it with minimal training.

As a pianist and music teacher, I had been very discouraged by my students' inability to read, analyze, memorize, and learn music at anything other than a snail's pace. Concluding that something was wrong with their early training, I determined to do something about it.

In 1965 I heard about Mary Helen Richards and attended a two-day workshop in Syracuse, New York, immediately recognizing that in her Kodály-inspired presentation was a possible solution to the problem of musical illiteracy. Mary Helen Richards was going to meet Kodály, who was composer-in-residence in the summer of 1965 at Dartmouth College's Hopkins Center in Hanover, New Hampshire. In exchange for transportation to New Hampshire, Mrs. Richards agreed to introduce me to Kodály. It was the first of three occasions when I was to meet him. Those encounters changed my life and resulted in my decision to go to Hungary and learn Kodály's way for myself.

I was in Budapest only three weeks before I realized that what I had learned from Mary Helen Richards and taught successfully at the Dana School of Music was barely the tip of the iceberg. I was determined to investigate every aspect of Hungarian music education, to study its superstructure, to learn the Kodály way of solfege and pedagogy as thoroughly as possible, and to bring a qualified Hungarian back to help me experiment with this remarkable system in the United States. Hungarian teachers whose names are almost legendary in America today opened their homes and hearts to me and helped me to achieve my purpose: Professor Erzsébet Szönyi, then dean of the Liszt Academy's choir conducting (music education) faculty; Márta Nemesszeghy; Helga Szabó; Katalin Forrai and László Vikár; Melinda Kistétényi, Erzsébet Hegyi and her husband, Dezsö Legány; Klára Kokas; Maria Katanics; Ildikó Herboly; Anikó Hamvás; and many others.

At the Liszt Academy I attended solfege classes of all five years simultaneously; not only did I wish to see how the classes built musicianship, but I was also seriously engaged in studying and doing the homework in Professor Szönyi's third-, fourth-, and fifth-year classes. I observed music classes in many cities and towns at all grade levels, from preschool to advanced teacher-training colleges. I discussed pedagogy with those who were responsible for the textbooks then in use at various age levels, and Márta Nemesszeghy even graciously allowed me to copy her first-grade curriculum lesson plans, day by day, as a guide to my first efforts at adaptation in the United States. I even talked with the head of the Országos Pedagógia Intézet (National Pedagogical Institute), the agency responsible for the overall curriculum in Hungary's total educational process. I wanted to know whether Dr. Szarka, the head of that agency, thought it possible to transplant and adapt Kodály's way of music education in a Western country. He replied that it would depend on the educational objectives of the country's government and on how much its citizens valued music as a part of any person's complete education. He implied that in Hungary the government considered music a key subject of the core curriculum, in that it helped to educate intellectually, emotionally, aesthetically, morally, politically, and even physically. I left that interview inspired by my contact with a society that valued music so highly, but discouraged by the unlikely prospect of our government at home ever according music so high a place in the educational process.

In spite of the inspiration received and the knowledge gained from my year's study in Hungary, as the time drew near to return home, I felt at a loss as to how to proceed to bring this marvelous way of music education to the United States. I sought the advice of both Professor Szönyi and Mrs. Kodály. What should I do? Train children or train teachers? Professor Szönyi said I should train teachers; Mrs. Kodály agreed, but said I must simultaneously create a model with children for prospective teachers to observe and follow. The notion that I could do both alone was preposterous. I had never taught in a public school or taught any general music classes — I was primarily a pianist and piano teacher. Mrs. Kodály told me I must take home a Hungarian to help me, but only the best-qualified, most highly respected and experienced teacher — one who had worked with her husband and knew his ideas.

Then began one of the most agonizing experiences of my Hungarian sojourn and entire career — trying to explain to Hungarian officials what I wanted and why, and trying to come to terms on which teacher I would be permitted to take. Not only was my ability to express myself in Hungarian inadequate, but in 1967–68 there was not the freedom of intercultural academic exchange that exists today. From a Hungarian viewpoint, it was a preposterous idea to send a Hungarian music teacher out of the country. Why should anyone want one anyway? Music education in Hungary was an accepted fact of the educational process; it was not known as the "Kodály method." It was simply the music curriculum supported by the Hungarian government. Why should I want to take it to the United States? I was either considered some kind of nut or suspected of having an ulterior motive. Officials were in conference, out to lunch, on vacation, or sick in bed when I tried to make appointments to discuss it. In those days Hungarian officials did not deal with private American ladies — they dealt only with governments or with the Ford Foundation, which, they intimated, was nearly the same as a government — a remark that later prompted me to submit a proposal to that foundation.

Though I persisted in my efforts, it became clear that officials had no intention of allowing me to bring any of the group who had worked with Kodály — they were "too valuable at home."‡ One day Mrs. Sára Takács, the administrative director of the Liszt Academy, made a suggestion that I offer to bring out a young man who was just graduating from the Academy, who was not yet employed, and for whom it would therefore not be so difficult to get permission to be released from his position, since he as yet had none. His name was Péter Erdei. I knew this young man well, since I had been attending his solfege class and had arranged to give him English lessons in exchange for his teaching me Hungarian musi-

‡The Ministry's official reason — the real reason, of course, being that those around Kodály were against the regime and, as such, not to be trusted out of the country.

cal terminology and answering my many questions about solfege. I was delighted with the idea but had not counted on Mrs. Kodály's reaction. She had never heard of Péter Erdei and maintained I must take only an experienced teacher. It was clearly a dilemma: the ministry would not let anyone experienced go, yet I needed Mrs. Kodály's support for my future efforts. I therefore determined to persuade her of Péter's abilities. She finally agreed to come to his diploma concert to see for herself. Among other works, Péter, ill with a high fever, conducted Kodály's *Jesus and the Traders* with great passion, precision, and dramatic intensity. Mrs. Kodály admitted that his was a strong talent and agreed that perhaps I could take him to the United States. Weeks of waiting followed, and just as I was about to give up and to leave the country in July, permission was suddenly granted. I shudder now to think what the result might be today had I been forced to come home and try to develop this gigantic concept by myself. I am convinced that the sudden capitulation of ministry officials to my nagging requests was an act of fate. It so nearly didn't happen at all.

My battle with American immigration authorities is another story — far worse than any dealings I had had with Hungarian officials. I had managed, through correspondence with Mrs. Edith Phelps, the principal of Dana Hall, to get Péter a part-time job directing the chapel choir at the school, where I was head of the music department.* But the immigration authorities in Boston could not understand why we took Mr. Erdei to be a person of "distinguished merit and ability," which he had to be in order to be admitted to the United States and to take a job away from another American. The typically narrow-minded and bureaucratic battl-ax with whom I had to deal in the Boston immigration office had never heard of Kodály and announced loudly that American music education was the best in the world — she knew, because her sister taught music

*Had ministry officials realized the religious nature of the Dana Hall choir, they most certainly would have refused to let him out of the country. Fortunately, the word *choir* in Hungary is synonymous with *glee club* or *chorus* in the United States. Since choirs in Hungary sing only secular music, I was perfectly safe in telling the ministry that Mr. Erdei's job would be to direct the Dana Hall choir.

[29]

in the Melrose school system (which at that time was no particular model of excellence), and why did I want to bring in some foreigner when we already had the best? It took practically an act of Congress to get around her. A somewhat nervous and apprehensive Péter finally arrived, nearly one month late.

Not only was everything new and strange for Péter Erdei, but there were also a host of problems in trying to decide where and how to begin our experiments with Kodály's way of music education. Péter and I laid out a plan that allowed us to devote our mornings to the Kodály work and our afternoons to our Dana Hall duties. In order to have enough time to experiment, I had renounced half of my position as the head of Dana Hall's music department and the Dana School of Music.

Our grand design included research to prove the validity of our experiments. Both Péter and I were woefully ignorant of scientifically controlled research procedures; I had been primarily a pianist and a teacher, not a scholar of education, and as far as Péter was concerned, American-style musical research was virtually unknown in Hungary. No one was directing our efforts; we were operating under no federal or foundation grants and were accountable to no organization or anything other than our own consciences. In short, we went blithely ahead, not realizing what we didn't know, stepping in where angels fear to tread. If neither of us knew anything about research, there was an even graver problem: neither of us knew anything about the American public school system — understandable in Péter's case, and as for me, I had attended and taught in private schools all my life. Nevertheless, I had realized in Hungary that since Kodály's system was based on the idea of music for *every* child, in order to be successful in the United States it would first have to be proven usable in the public schools.

I had been fortunate in finding a nearby school system in Winchester, Massachusetts, that was willing to provide the three schools with the three sets of first grades we had decided were necessary to compare the results of daily and weekly Kodály and traditional music teaching. Today it would be nearly impossible — in the Northeast at least — to find a school system that would allow a daily music class, but in 1968 the "back to basics" movement had not yet taken hold, and the Kodály system was new and untried; people were curious about it. Thus we found our experimental school system quite easily.

Our next step was to visit local public schools to acquaint Péter with the atmosphere of American classrooms, the general characteristics of American children, and some aspects of traditional American music education. Péter was appalled: first, at the clutter on the walls and in every nook and cranny of the classrooms, which were often replete with hamsters, rabbits, or white mice; second, at the undisciplined behavior of American children; and third, at the dull, lifeless material they were receiving in music class and their inability to match even faintly the pitch of any song they were singing. I think he was ready to take the next plane back to Hungary! With some degree of shock, I realized I was nearly as appalled as he was — it had never occurred to me that music education could be so poor in an affluent suburb of Boston, a city that was supposed to be the seat of American culture and that boasted the finest universities, symphony orchestras, opera, and ballet.

Before we could begin our experimental teaching in the Winchester public schools, we had to find suitable American songs for first-grade use. Péter researched hundreds of books, taken from the Boston Public Library or Harvard's Widener Library. He found many beautiful songs — almost all of them too difficult for the first-grade level. In one year's time, after looking at thousands of songs, he came up with only thirty-five he felt were both authentic and of good quality. Fortunately, we needed only two or three new songs a week, so we were just able to meet our own demands.

Though I had visited László Vikár several times at the Hungarian Academy of Sciences during my year in Hungary, had seen Kodály's and Bartók's original collection of folk songs, and discussed the ongoing work of the folk music research group there, I was pitifully ignorant of the task that faced us in preparation for our first teaching experiments. I did not understand why we could not simply pick some not too difficult songs with suitable texts for first-grade children from existing folk song collections. I did not realize that selection involved far more than methodological considerations (that is, finding enough so-mi or ta ti-ti ta songs to begin first-grade teaching), or even considerations of musical taste; but Péter knew the importance of following Bartók's and Kodály's intent — namely, to identify, develop, and ultimately preserve a national culture. It was not until some two months had passed and I had witnessed Péter's daily shifts from gloom to elation as he had either found or not found a new song he considered worthy that I realized he was already committed to the same procedures Kodály and Bartók had used in developing the *Corpus Musicae Popularis Hungaricae*. Their original plan of coming up with five to six thousand songs that would survive critical examination, and that would then be analyzed and catalogued systematically according to types and characteristics, was a guiding light to Péter and something he intended to emulate. That meant looking at a hundred songs for every one ultimately chosen. When I finally realized his intentions, the magnitude of the task seemed overwhelming, until I remembered Kodály's words to me at Stanford University in 1966. Comparing the tiny country of Hungary with our huge United States (which I suggested was more like fifty countries), I had asked how we could possibly proceed to identify our national cultural heritage. He replied optimistically and enthusiastically: "Why, you have the richest possibilities in the world with your vast melting pot of cultures."

Péter clearly felt we had to collect all types and variations, from all of North America's geographical areas and from all of the ethnic groups settled in them. Our immediate task at hand was to teach upper-middle-class suburban children living in New England, but Péter was already building for the future — he was equally excited to find songs from North Carolina, Louisiana, Nova Scotia, or Vermont.

At first we did not realize how much work had already been done. As a pianist who had become interested in education, I had had no particular interest in folk music and was not aware of the work of such collectors as Alan Lomax and Charles C. Brown, or of the wax cylinders in the attic of the Library of Congress. Péter soon located many sources in his research efforts; he found that there already existed a great wealth of both published and unpublished material. Even having identified such material, however, we were still faced with the problem of how to sequence and build a methodology from it. Looking back on developments in the United States and Canada, I know now what a great debt of gratitude the American Kodály movement owes to Péter Erdei and, soon to join him, to Katalin Komlós, who continued and expanded his early work, which ultimately resulted in publication of the collection 150 *American Folk Songs to Sing, Read and Play* (Boosey and Hawkes, 1974), systematically arranged according to Bartók's and Kodály's system, and chosen for the express purpose of use in American schools. Without their vision, their insistence on a firm base, and their choice of only the most excellent and valuable material, the whole American Kodály movement might have rested on a faulty foundation. By and large, Americans have never been noted for a discriminating sense of taste in cultural matters — a taste that is now deteriorating because of hard rock, television, and commercialization. That the authentic Kodály movement nevertheless has had a significant impact on traditional American music education and on other systems, such as Orff Schulwerk, is both inescapable fact and happy consequence. Authentic and good-quality folk music is becoming established as a cornerstone of elementary American music education, in spite of the infiltration of the rock-pop culture.

Péter and I began our Winchester experiments that winter of 1968 with altogether too few songs; we were indeed quite desperate for suitable material. Every morning we drove to Winchester together — about a fifty-minute drive. Péter, whose objective had been to teach at the high school level when he finished the Liszt Academy, had severe doubts about teaching first-grade children. He was an immediate success however; the children adored him, and their regular classroom teacher was astonished at their progress.

Following my observation of Péter's daily first-grade lesson, I taught a twice-weekly first-grade Kodály lesson. It is one thing to observe beautiful teaching such as Péter Erdei's, or to understand it intellectually; it is another to put it into practice in the classroom.

Though I was old enough be Péter's mother and was technically his employer, I suffered severe agony at the thought of his observing my teaching. On the ride back from Winchester to Wellesley, Péter would evaluate my lesson and analyze all the mistakes I had made, gently instructing me how I could have done it better.

Simultaneously with the Winchester teaching, I taught a pilot class of third- to sixth-graders from the public schools of the Wellesley community, twice weekly from 5 to 6 P.M. Originally started for experimental purposes at the Dana School of Music before I had gone to Hungary, the class had been exposed first to Orff techniques (in which I had become interested in 1963, before my introduction to Kodály's ideas)† and to Mary Helen Richards–type Kodály. When I returned from Hungary in the fall of 1968, I taught this class with my new Kodály knowledge; Péter observed me, evaluated my teaching, and sometimes taught the class himself. It is important to give at least a brief summary of the class's development, because it came to play a significant role in the early development of the American Kodály movement.

In February 1969, about six months after Péter Erdei arrived in the United States, we took the class to the Eastern Division meeting of the Music Educators National Conference in Washington, D.C. There, before an audience of thirteen hundred educators, the students demonstrated Kodály literacy skills, sang simple two- and three-part a cappella art music, and performed artistic arrangements of folk songs and composed art songs, accompanying themselves and also improvising on a small ensemble of Orff instruments. The accomplishments of this class burst on the astonished audience of music educators, who apparently were incredulous to learn that ordinary public school children could produce such results. Because they had used the Orff instruments, the term "Orff-Kodály method"

---

†Members of the staff at the Dana School of Music had been introduced to the Orff approach by Grace Nash, who gave several successful summer workshops on our campus in the early 1960s. While in Europe I also spent the month of January 1968 in Germany and Austria studying the Orff approach, and I returned to the Orff Institute in July to attend the English-language Orff workshop there. See "Kodály and Orff: Report from Europe," *Music Educators Journal*, April 1969.

[34]

was born — much to my distress, since while each system (Orff and Kodály) is a separate and beautiful thing in itself, neither composer envisioned a "method" and certainly not a combination of their two approaches into a synthesized curriculum.‡

The class subsequently gave a similar demonstration in New Haven, Connecticut, at a large conference aimed at improving that city's overall education, with the result that educational authorities there decided they must have this new Kodály approach for New Haven's music program. It was a tremendous opportunity. Though authorities tried their best to convince us to come to New Haven, we could not have helped them at that point, since we had no trained music teachers as yet to send them. However, I knew that Professor Alexander Ringer, a musicologist at the University of Illinois at Urbana who had met Kodály and become interested in his way of music education, had sent ten young music teachers to study in Hungary on a National Endowment grant and that he was looking for cities where they could develop a daily curriculum upon their return to the United States. It was like an answer to a prayer. I was able to put this group in contact with New Haven authorities, with the result that most of the Ringer group went to New Haven and developed there a strong Kodály program, which continues today.

In the spring of 1970 my pilot class traveled to Hungary to spend ten days in Kecskemét and another week in Budapest to make a

‡A few months later I announced my intention to cease my work with the Orff approach: "Shortly after I first became interested in the Kodály concept in 1965, I advocated the combining of the two concepts. . . . When I first started my pilot class three years ago, I taught it mostly Orff. . . . What happened this fall [1968] was that, when I saw the literacy and musicianship being developed in these children by the Kodály, I nearly abandoned the Orff. . . .

"When I was in Salzburg, Dr. Herman Regner, the director of the Orff Institute, convinced me of the importance of knowing the Orff at the source and of studying it in depth. I must concede that he is right. . . . Yet if I spent the rest of my life trying to establish the Kodály in this country, there still would not be time enough. . . . I am, therefore, regretfully announcing that my active involvement in the Orff movement must be largely curtailed, though my interest in it and my support of it will in no way be diminished" ("Orff and Kodály: Catalysts for Change," speech delivered at the Dana School of Music's Orff and Kodály Teacher Training Workshop, 1969).

film with the children of the Kecskemét Kodály school to prove that American children could indeed achieve a standard of musical literacy similar to that of Hungarian children. That film, *Let's Sing Together*, made by Gábor Takács at MA Film, was first shown in Moscow in the summer of 1970 at the ISME conference, at the first Kodály seminar in Kecskemét in the same summer, and subsequently in the early 1970s at several American universities. It created a sensation because the college music students who observed it did not believe these far younger children could do such things as hear in their heads, read at sight, take dictation, and perform two- and three-part music a cappella in tune, things they themselves could not do — in fact, it often angered them, because they felt they had been cheated in their own music education.

Parenthetically, in the summer of 1980, ten years after the film was made, a reunion of that class was held at the Kodály Center of America's summer course. We heard from all twenty-two members — most of them by then either graduating or just graduated from college and spread as far away as Texas. Eleven attended the reunion and demonstrated that they still remembered everything they had learned.*

To return to our Winchester story — at the end of Péter Erdei's and my first year of experimentation in the Winchester public schools, I organized a six-week summer course at the Dana School of Music, where the first Hungarian teachers to come to the United States taught and lectured. Those who came were Professor Szőnyi, Katalin Forrai, László Vikár, and Klára Kokas.† I felt that these four could give us a good picture of Hungarian music education

---

*Since this article was written, three members of the class have graduated from well-known conservatories and music schools. One is teaching at New England Conservatory and directs the Massachusetts Junior Youth Ensemble; one has earned a Ph.D. from the University of Michigan and is teaching at the Eastman School of Music; one is a graduate of the KCA Academic Year program and is teaching at the Dana School of Music, where she first joined the pilot class in the third grade; and another won the 1992 Sarolta Kodály Scholarship to study in Kecskemét and has just returned from a year there. All twenty-two were actively involved in amateur music organizations at the time of the 1980 reunion.

†Orff experts from Salzburg also taught at the 1969 summer course; see "A New Dimension," closing speech at the 1986 summer session, Kecskemét, Hungary.

and the problems we would have in developing it, since they were leaders in fields important to our purposes: teacher training, preschool, folk music, and educational research.

It was an historic course, and many who attended it have had a significant influence on the development of the North American Kodály movement today — among them Sean Deibler, Sr. Mary Alice Hein, Toni Locke, and Faith Knowles; Betsy Moll and Lois Choksy did not take the course but came to visit.‡ Choksy had felt that the Kodály method was much overrated and would present too many problems to be successfully adapted in our type of society. What she saw at that course changed her mind and life; after observing the teaching of the four Hungarians and Péter Erdei's second-grade demonstration class, she admitted that her misconceptions had been based on too little and nonauthentic information. As a result of her visit, she decided to go to Hungary and investigate Kodály's "method" for herself.

Near the end of the course a surprise telephone call informed me that my proposal to the Ford Foundation had been accepted and that a large grant would soon enable me to establish an institute to train teachers in the Kodály method — if I could find at least four

‡Sean Deibler established a model Kodály class at the Haverford School in Pennsylvania in the same year. He later became the first American Kodály master teacher. He has earned a fine reputation as a choral and instrumental conductor in both American and European concert halls, frequently performing new and challenging works. Sr. Mary Alice Hein, of Holy Names College, went on to attend the 1970 summer courses at Esztergom and Kecskemét, then broke her original connection with Mary Helen Richards to establish an authentic model class at Saint Theresa's Parochial School in Oakland, California (see "The Kodály Concept in the U.S.," *Hungarian Quarterly*, Autumn 1976). She soon developed a highly successful Kodály program at Holy Names and organized the first international Kodály symposium there in 1973; this symposium was instrumental in creating the International Kodály Society, founded at Kecskemét in 1975. Toni Locke, a member of KMTI's first graduating class, helped to develop the Holy Names program; an outstanding musicologist, she is editor of the highly acclaimed song collection *Sail Away*. Lois Choksy, whose earlier career included Kodály teaching in Baltimore Public Schools and Holy Names College, is now head of the Kodály program at the University of Calgary in Alberta, Canada. She is the author of several books based on the Kodály concept. Faith Knowles is currently Associate Director of KCA.

teachers and be ready to start in September. It was then August. I was overwhelmed. I had made the proposal earlier the same year but had never really believed it would be funded. The program officer who was responsible for recommending the grant to the Ford trustees said that my pilot class had convinced him that American children should have the opportunity to learn this method. In any case, I had to act in a big hurry. Fortunately, I had taken the precaution of notifying Dana Hall of my intention to resign if the grant were to materialize. On the last day of the summer course I announced the good news to the participants and said I needed four students immediately. We had no trouble getting them, since their tuition and expenses were completely paid by the grant.*

Following the course, when Péter and I should have been on vacation, we went into a wild flurry of activity instead. We met with Professor Szönyi before she left for Hungary to ask her advice on what kind of a program we should have for our first students. We were like babes in the woods. We had no building, no furniture, no program, no secretary, and no one to help us. But we had $184,000, four students, and about fifty good first-grade American folk songs. Professor Szönyi was extremely helpful and even found a business manager for our new Institute.†

The next thing we did was to invite Mrs. Kodály and Márta Nemesszeghy, then director of the Kodály School in Kecskemét, to come to the United States for six weeks to help us to make a long-range plan for the Institute. Fortunately for us, they accepted. Because we had no building until November, we started in my own home. We put our four students to work in the basement researching folk songs, while Mrs. Kodály, Mrs. Nemesszeghy, Péter, and I spent long hours at the dining room table trying to decide how best to start: what to teach, how long the training should take, what recognition would be offered (whether certificate or diploma), how

---

*KMTI's first four students were Toni Locke, Keith Knighton, Jane Thurber, and Lee Robbins (Carter).

†Zoltán Tomory, a friend who had been in prison with Professor Szönyi's husband during the war, had later emigrated to this country, and was working at Harvard.

to spread the idea, where to locate the Institute.‡ We had invitations to establish the Institute in many places, and all four of us visited West Hartford, New Haven, and New York to investigate the possibilities. In the end we decided to develop the Institute in the Boston area so I could keep my pilot class and so Péter could continue his work with the Dana Hall choir, at least temporarily.

Meanwhile, we also continued to teach classes in Winchester, so that our four students would have a model to observe. We had almost no time to plan and organize, we really were not ready to start training teachers, but we started anyway, because the grant stipulated that we start immediately. I'm afraid our first four students were quite upset with us, because we were so busy making plans, trying to find a suitable building, and teaching the first- and second-grade classes, which were to be the model, that we could not give them our full attention.

At first the Institute was called the Kodály Center. When we became legally incorporated after several months, the name was changed to the Kodály Musical Training Institute (KMTI). Péter and I had many problems that first year, because every step was new and we often had to fail before we could succeed. The year was over before we knew it, and much remained to be done before the Institute could be said to be established. To add to our problems, when news first spread of the Ford grant, everyone was suddenly inter-

‡ I described our curriculum in a report at the Music Educators Conference at Győr, Hungary, June 19, 1971, as follows: "We now have a two-year teacher-training course that gives a diploma; the first year of study is in the United States, the second year in Hungary. The teachers in this course already have American degrees in music but want to be retrained in the Kodály method. They study solfege, conducting, Hungarian language, American folk music, and Kodály methodology, and they observe and practice-teach in our model schools. After they return from the year of study in Hungary, which is divided between the Kecskemét music/primary school, the Liszt Academy, and other schools in Budapest, we place them for a third year in one of our model schools to help them over the first year of teaching the Kodály method. . . . Our first graduating class of three teachers has just returned from Hungary and received its diplomas; last September we enrolled nine teachers, seven of whom will come to Hungary this fall."

ested. People wanted to know who was Kodály and what was his method; how could one go to Hungary; could I advise them what to see and help them to go there; and above all, could they get any money from our Ford grant to go? Everyone assumed that because we had a Ford Foundation grant we had money to give away. Such was not the case, as anyone who has dealt with that foundation knows; every penny must be accounted for *before* the grant is approved. Nonetheless, we were swamped with requests, and many of the names familiar to Americans and Canadians in the Kodály movement today are people for whom I hastily made arrangements and tried to open doors, excitedly telling them everything I knew and had seen in Hungary, urging them to go there to see for themselves.

In the summer of 1970, the first Kecskemét summer seminar for foreigners was held. Péter did not teach in it, but he brought his Dana Hall choir to perform at the opening. They also performed Kodály's *Angels and the Shepherds* with Ilona Andor's beautiful choir — her choir singing in Hungarian and Péter's in English, if you can imagine such a thing! In any case, it was so successful that it had to be repeated, now with Péter conducting the two choirs, quaking in his boots to be conducting Ilona Andor's famous choir without rehearsal and with her watching.

Twenty-six Americans attended that first Kecskemét seminar in 1970 — all but one from the 1969 Dana School of Music Summer Course. Our original intention was to alternate courses between the two countries, one summer in one country, the next in the other.* It happened that way from 1969 to 1974, but in 1974 — when the course should have been in Kecskemét — the new home of the

---

*"In the summer of 1971 we held our ... summer course at the University of Bridgeport, Connecticut, which was attended by seventy-five Americans and Canadians, among them Mae Daly [who later established the Kodály Institute of Canada]. Since 1973 we have held our summer course at Wellesley College" ("Report to Canada," paper read at the National Kodály Conference, Vancouver, British Columbia, 1976). I related a remarkable incident from that 1971 summer course in "The Why of Kodály" (*Music Journal*, September 1971): "One evening offered a superb performance by Saint Catherine's Choir (girls aged twelve to sixteen) from Blackpool, England (conducted by Margaret Holden). The audi-

Zoltán Kodály Pedagogical Institute was in process of being built and was not yet ready, so the course was again held in Wellesley. By that time, KMTI was offering a certificate for a Kodály program followed only in the United States, and, since the demand for training was growing and many people could not afford to travel to Hungary, it became necessary to offer a U.S. summer course every summer.

The development of the American Kodály movement, and of the international movement as well, is indebted to Péter Erdei's early work and that of the first Hungarians who followed: Klára Kokas, Éva Rozgonyi, Éva Vendrei, and Helga Szabó. Péter stayed in the United States for four years and has continued to come summers at least every other year, when he is not directing an international course in Kecskemét, where he was appointed director of the Institute in 1974. During the four years he helped me to build the Kodály Musical Training Institute, many things were accomplished. In addition to producing 150 *American Folk Songs* with Kati Komlós, Péter advised and helped me with the small books I had already written or was in the process of writing; together we made the plan for the pilot class film; he also made a videotape with second-grade children in Needham, Massachusetts, that is still in demand by American colleges for their music methodology classes. His far-sighted vision always led him to think ten years ahead, to foresee problems, to anticipate outcomes. Before he left, we had managed: (1) to establish, in 1971, an affiliation with the New England Con-

---

ence left the hall transformed. The choir, which had had daily training in the Kodály concept for two years, walked back to the new dormitory that housed the participants of the workshop. As they stood waiting for their bus they began to sing again, spontaneously, without a conductor. They gave a totally different program; their repertoire seemed inexhaustible. They sang everything from Palestrina to Britten. When they did not know the words, they sang in sol-fa. They could not be stopped, though the bus awaited them. One favorite piece by Kodály, *Táncnóta*, they sang six times during the hour! The rest of us stood listening, mesmerized, caught up in the incredible feeling of the moment; for these children were lost in the beauty of the music, and we all realized that they had received something priceless and which is theirs now for a lifetime. It is our task to see that the lives of increasing numbers of youth may be so enriched."

servatory of Music for the granting of a master's degree with Kodály emphasis; (2) to begin the implementation of a six-year plan in Needham, a suburb of Boston, that would produce a sequential curriculum; (3) to establish model schools in inner-city Boston; and (4) to lay the base for further dissemination of the Kodály concept through the designing of a program for West Hartford, Connecticut, which was to become the Institute's pilot city, according to plans laid out earlier with Mrs. Kodály and Mrs. Nemesszeghy.†

The academic-musical program that Professor Szönyi, Péter, and I originally laid out together, and that was then approved by Mrs. Kodály and Mrs. Nemesszeghy and finally taught by Péter — alone the first year, later by other Hungarians who came to join him — is basically the same program we teach today. Its structure is so sound that it can be added to or subtracted from according to any given teaching environment without losing its essence — and here it is important to say that it was Péter who taught me to think always in terms of the music and of Kodály's overall philosophy of education rather than the methodology alone. It is this emphasis that has enabled us to adapt the Kodály concept in America. Had we tried to adapt merely the methodology, we would have been doomed before we began. Yet the clever tricks and gimmicks, assumed to be the methodology and apparently leading to quick success, are what most teachers think they want when they first hear about the Kodály concept. But can you imagine teaching a methodology that will equally embrace African Americans, Hispanics, Asians, American Indians, and many other ethnic groups?

Very early in our adaptation efforts, Péter saw that there would be a problem with Americans in "going overboard" with this matter of methodology, and also of folk song. Americans tend to want the answers to everything overnight; we seize upon anything new with energy and intensity, but frequently we lack the depth of understanding, commitment, and patience to build slowly, thoroughly,

†KMTI arranged with the Hungarian Ministry for a gifted young Hungarian, Klára Nemes, to develop the program. A nearby town, Bloomfield, Connecticut, later asked for and received a Hungarian master teacher, Maria Mihálovics.

and excellently. We are too prone to be satisfied with superficial knowledge. Although folk song is far from superficial, it is only half the story — the other half is the art music to which folk music is the stepping-stone. Many American teachers are content never to go to a concert again, once they have received that precious piece of paper — the bachelor's degree — which allows them to teach. This is the fault of our American system of music education, which values practical preparation for employment far above individual personal fulfillment. Péter was determined that this should not be the case with the Kodály concept in America. From the beginning he stressed the importance and the goal of art music — the participation in live music making. It has not been easy for American teachers to reorient their thinking to such a goal, for it means bringing them into a closer relationship with performers and live performance, which is not a traditional situation for either teachers or performers in any country, but one that is at the heart of Kodály's philosophy.

No history of the early years of the American Kodály movement can be complete without making reference to the fine achievements of many others in the movement. As a result of their dedication and hard work we now have an increasing number of institutions where one can get Kodály training under the guidance of people who took the trouble to observe and learn at the source in Hungary.‡ They are spread from Texas to California through the work of Mark Williams and Sr. Mary Alice Hein; from Alabama to Wisconsin through Barbara Kaplan and Sr. Lorna Zemke; from Pittsburgh to Indiana through Betsy Moll and Jean Sinor; and from one coast of Canada to the other by pioneers such as Mae Daly, Shirley Blakely and Vernon Ellis, Pierre Perron, Ann Osborne, John Young, and more recently, Lois Choksy. Many others are too numerous to

‡Institutions that have offered or currently offer master's degrees with Kodály emphasis, besides those mentioned elsewhere in this chapter, include Holy Names College in California; Hartt School of Music, West Hartford, Connecticut; the University of Connecticut at Storrs; American and Catholic Universities, Washington, D.C.; Ithaca College, Ithaca, New York; and the Cincinnati Conservatory of Music.

mention but no less important. And the dissemination grows ever wider through the teachers who have attended or are attending courses at U.S. institutions offering in-depth Kodály programs. The graduates and summer course participants of the two institutions I founded in Kodály's name* are teaching in over forty of our fifty states and eleven foreign countries. Some of them, those who have followed our two-year diploma course, have been to Hungary to study, but they are too few. They are like fine gold now, those who have both the American and Hungarian training and who have become the master teachers to train others. We must train many more.

The fourteen years since Péter Erdei and I started in the United States have seen a significant development and spread of the Kodály concept. We threw a pebble into a huge lake, which quickly sent ripples in ever-widening circles.† What was at first merely an innovative idea has become a movement that has permeated the fabric of our society. It could not have been accomplished without the help, concern, and investment of a great amount of time and effort

*My departure from KMTI and founding of the Kodály Center of America in 1977 is detailed later in this book, in "The Challenge of Change."

†An amusing example of the Kodály concept's assimilation into American culture is the 1977 film *Close Encounters of the Third Kind*. I described the genesis of that film in my speech "Communication and the Kodály Concept," given at the Hunter Art Museum, Chattanooga, Tennessee, January 10, 1978: "Steven Spielberg, who wrote and directed the film, knew that he wanted music to be the means of communication between Earth and the other planet. When Spielberg was looking for the exact vehicle to accomplish his purpose, it was Douglass Trumbull, creator of the film's special effects, who told Spielberg to look into the Kodály concept. This resulted in our sending a faculty member, Floice Lindgren, to Alabama to explain the Kodály concept to Spielberg. My first reaction to using the Kodály concept in the film was negative: I feared that it would stress only the gimmicks and tools of the method and, if poorly done, would only result in bad publicity and damage to the Kodály movement. It is ironic that it should have been those very tools (the hand signals and the language of sol-fa) that were responsible for getting across the essence of the Kodály philosophy and relating it to Spielberg's message that music is a universal means of communication."

on the part of many Hungarians, both those who were pioneers in laying the foundations for the KMTI's first experimental efforts and in disseminating them through the early summer courses, and later those who helped me to establish a second institution — the Kodály Center of America (KCA). These Hungarians established teaching principles so firmly based on Kodály's philosophy that the concept has been able to survive the fate of many other musical ideologies now consigned to the trash heap of history. Furthermore, they laid a very broad base: Kati Komlós made the model in the field of folk music research that has since been followed by many others; Klára Kokas made the first model with black children in inner-city schools (without which we would have fallen flat on our faces) and also laid the foundation for our educational research efforts; Éva Rozgonyi's pioneering work with learning-disabled children gave us the courage, ten years later, to attempt an important pilot project that would document the effectiveness of a Kodály program with such children through educational research.

When Péter Erdei returned to Hungary after four years, I felt very much alone and wondered if I would be able to make the necessary decisions to direct the Institute's affairs by myself. At that point Helga Szabó and Éva Vendrei arrived to help me make the transition, and Helga coordinated the faculty's efforts, which resulted in the curriculum guidebook *Kodály for Beginning Levels*. She later produced an American version of *Te Is Tudsz Énekelni*, called *You Can Sing Too*, for use with very young children by parents and nonmusician classroom teachers.‡ Kati Forrai gave our American faculty the basic guidelines in how to work with preschool children, and Erzsébet Hegyi laid the foundation for training college-level teachers how to teach solfege, both in courses and through the book I asked her to write for American use but that was eventually published by the Kecskemét Kodály Institute — *Solfege According to the Kodály Concept*. Klára Nemes developed the first large-scale program in another large city

‡A book many years ahead of its time, since it is only recently that American educators, and especially music educators, have come to realize the vital importance of early childhood education.

— West Hartford, where the teachers knew nothing about Kodály. She had to train them from the beginning through in-service courses at the same time they were teaching.*

One day a book publicly recognizing all those Hungarians who came to work under my direction at either the Kodály Musical Training Institute or the Kodály Center of America must be written, for they were instrumental in building the American Kodály movement. Everything I have written here is only part of the story, for the history is still being made, not only in my country, but in many other parts of the world. As Kodály said, "We must look forward to the time when all peoples in all lands are brought together through singing, and when there is a universal harmony." [1] The membership of the International Kodály Society, which is composed of students, teachers, performing artists, composers, and social scientists from over thirty-four countries of the world, in less than one generation since its founding in 1975, is testimony to the greatness of Kodály's ideas. I think he would be happy to know the result of his more than fifty years of labor in behalf of his own country and mankind. What has been accomplished toward Kodály's goal since he left us is not perfect — it is not yet even excellent — and we must never cease to strive for that goal.

[1] Zoltán Kodály, *Selected Writings* (Budapest: Corvina Press, 1974), p. 215.

---

*Klára Nemes also helped to develop a similar project in Chattanooga, Tennessee, where she spent an academic year developing a pilot program and helping those teachers who had been sent to KCA's summer course under the terms of a three-year Lyndhurst Foundation grant. The establishment of a Kodály music program in Chattanooga and Hamilton County, Tennessee, was the result of tireless efforts by Helen Bryan, a woman of extraordinary vision and true pioneering spirit, who insisted on bringing Hungarian experts to lay a foundation of excellence. Other Hungarians who helped to develop the program there were László Dobszay and Lilla Gábor; also, Albert Bradshaw of Ireland, and the Americans Sean Deibler and Lamar Robertson.

teaching must guard against the things that have turned off American music educators, and even Hungarian children, whenever a teacher is poorly trained or seizes upon only superficial appurtenances. We must not make a religion of folk music; it is only a basis and stepping-stone, not the be-all and end-all of music education. Nor must we make the development of musical literacy the primary goal, because that way can sow the seeds of our own destruction: I refer to the emphasis on methodology over music and the dull repetition of mechanical drill over the joyous experience of performing and creating music because a child has both consciously and unconsciously acquired the tools to do so.

KCA'S FIRST TEN YEARS

Where does our small Center, KCA, fit into the national and international picture I have been describing? When we founded the Center in 1977, our purposes in establishing a new institution were as follows:

1. To remain an independent institution, and thus be able to dictate our own policies and maintain a quality standard.
2. To remain in contact with the original source in Hungary, which was the model of excellence on which we needed to build and from which we can still learn.
3. To remain on the cutting edge of innovation, and thus to experiment with those aspects of the Kodály concept that can be of service in fields other than music education.

The question now, after ten years, is, Are we carrying out these purposes? What I can say to answer this question is:

1. Yes, we have remained independent, with the result that we have acquired both a national and international reputation of excellence in Kodály-based teacher training.
2. Yes, we have remained in contact with the original source in Hungary and expanded our contacts there to include a new

generation of younger teachers who have been influenced by and who have built on the training they received from the previous generation of Kodály's own students. This continued cultural interchange has been one of the most valuable offerings of KCA to prospective music teachers; it is responsible for the education of the heart and spirit as well as of the mind, ear, voice, and hand.

3. Yes, we have remained on the cutting edge of innovation. We have become involved in work with learning-disabled children and with underprivileged minorities in both school settings and such environments as after-school and community centers. We are constantly seeking new avenues to demonstrate the value of music used in the Kodály way, as a vehicle to transcend the problems of daily existence, with populations ranging from infancy to senior citizens and, we hope, in the future, from those in nursing homes and prisons to those who are blind or deaf.

I believe it can be said that we have adhered to our purposes and remained true to our goals. The next question is, How well have we done? That is not so easy to answer. I often feel that our graduates are producing better results in their teaching careers than we ourselves at the Center. I'm not sure this is a bad thing. Isn't it, after all, what we want — to produce graduates of excellence who will make an impact and be successful wherever they go? We exist mainly to provide a model, to inspire a commitment to what is possible, and to point the way to get there.

Boston is undoubtedly the hardest place in the country to bring about any sort of change, to establish an institution, or to train teachers. The apathy that exists in educational circles here reflects the tenacity of the old notion that Boston is the "Hub of the Universe" — intellectually, culturally, socially, and economically. In ten years I have not yet succeeded in establishing a permanent relationship with any leading Boston musical institution. It appears that the success of the Kodály concept is a threat to both established and nontenured faculty. KCA-trained students and graduates have attempted to persuade their alma maters to establish a master's program with Kodály emphasis through KCA in Ohio, Pennsylvania, Virginia, and Texas, to name only a few, but with little success.

Given this fact, it would seem more sensible for graduates to try to get positions within those institutions themselves. That has already happened in some universities; in such cases, however, not only is the Kodály-trained teacher subject to institutional bureaucracy and politics, but Kodály-related courses may be only a small part of one's total course load.

I have often been asked why we don't move KCA from Boston to Kansas or some other less resistant setting. My answer is that one can find resistance to a greater or lesser degree anywhere and everywhere, and in any case we are committed to Boston's children, who very much need what we have to offer. It is up to us to overcome it.

KCA'S FUTURE: THE NEXT TEN YEARS

From the foregoing, one thing is clear. As of 1987, the institutions that can offer complete, in-depth training and a master's degree with Kodály emphasis are few and far between. Of those few that exist (Holy Names, KMTI, and KCA), KCA is the only totally independent one, able to say what its curriculum will be, who its faculty will be, and how much training will be required to receive a certificate or diploma.

This independence has been bought at a price: faculty and administrative salaries are too low, fund-raising is a time-consuming and exhausting challenge, and everyone — faculty, administration, the board of trustees — must make superhuman efforts just in order to hold on to what we already have, let alone plan for the exciting things we feel we should and can accomplish in the future.

Today one hears of mergers everywhere — airlines, telephone companies, banks, even educational institutions. It is hard to predict what will happen to KCA. The Kodály concept is now well established in the United States; it will survive whether KCA does or not. I am sometimes tempted to say to our board of trustees that it would be better to disband at the height of our reputation than to accede to the domination of a parent institution that could dictate our policies and standards.

What would be lost were we to take that route? In light of present economic conditions and the national expansion of the Kodály movement, is there still a role for us to play? What can we offer our students that can meet the competition of other, lower-costing summer and academic-year programs, less time commitment, easier practice-teaching requirements?

Although we may be unable to offer our academic-year students the very best model they will ever see (since many graduates are creating models better than we can possibly produce in the Boston school system), we can offer the chance to cope with problems as they are in the real world, under constant supervision and sympathetic guidance. Those graduates who have emerged intact (and they all have so far!) from a year of KCA-supervised teaching in a Boston public school say they feel equipped to teach anywhere in the world, and that they can meet any situation. In addition, we can offer our students, in both academic-year and summer courses, an in-depth musical education wherein the component parts — solfege, conducting, methodology, materials, and choral singing — are synthesized into a unified whole.

I believe KCA's future role is (1) to provide the highest standard of Kodály-based teacher training possible, and (2) to adapt as many of Kodály's philosophical ideas and musical techniques as are applicable to other musical markets — for instance, to applied music majors (performers) in colleges and universities and, at the opposite end of the scale, to classroom teachers in school systems that will never be able to afford trained music specialists. Above all, if we are to justify our reason for continued existence, we must constantly hold before us the goals of excellence, of quality music for use everywhere, of dignifying the profession of music teaching, and of attracting qualified teachers into it.

Such goals are not only for KCA as an institution but for all those whom we exist to serve. KCA's trustees, faculty, and administration

[54]

have committed themselves to working toward these goals together with students who are willing to make the same commitment.

I can promise you, from personal experience, that a lifetime devoted to making beautiful music accessible to one's fellow travelers in life — whether children or adults — can be one of the most meaningful careers to which one can aspire.

5. An End and a Beginning

This chapter is excerpted from the closing speech at KCA's 1989 summer course in Kecskemét — a speech I then thought would be my last.

This is the last speech I shall give as director of KCA since, as most of you know, I plan to retire officially from administration of that institution's programs and policies as of August 31 — only three weeks more to articulate my hopes and dreams for the future and to influence decisions concerning what directions our Center shall take.

In the last four weeks, a torrent of memories, reflections, questions, and ideas has crowded my brain and bombarded my heart. I realize now that much has happened and much has changed over the last two decades. Some answers have been found to problems I had anticipated in the United States, and the spread of the so-called Kodály method has been little short of phenomenal worldwide, but I feel, nonetheless, that teachers, parents, and educational and governmental authorities still do not grasp the importance of Kodály's legacy nor understand its implications.

Upon my return to the United States in 1968 following my year of study in Hungary, I was on fire with the notion that the Kodály concept could create a revolution in American music education. I wanted to build and raise the standard of musical taste of the general American public, and I wanted to start all over with teacher training from the ground up. How naïve I was then, and how full of good intentions! It never occurred to me that what

I considered very quiet and miniscule efforts could result in the controversy and factionalism that later developed.

My opening speech to those attending the now historic 1969 Dana School of Music Orff and Kodály Summer Course unwittingly started the controversy by stating that I was withdrawing from the Orff movement — not because I didn't approve of the Orff concept but because I could not develop both concepts in depth simultaneously, and because I felt the Kodály approach to be more important and basic to the development of a musically literate American public.*

I wanted the participants of that first summer course, whether interested in Orff or Kodály, to know why I was electing to devote all my energies to the development of Kodály's ideas. I said I did not know whether the "method" (which I now know is much more than a method, a term I no longer use) could or would be adapted in the United States, but that I could say why it *should* be adapted for our country's use.† I said people would have to discover what was and what was not the "method," and I urged my audience to look for the philosophy behind it. I expressed several concerns: for instance, could it work in a democracy, or in urban settings? Those

---

*That speech, "Can the Kodály Method Be Successfully Adapted Here?," was subsequently published in MUSART, April–May 1970.

†My strong position on the Kodály "method" in the early years was soon reversed. I believe now that what I was referring to as a "method" was actually the feeling for order and sequence that I had observed in the teaching of Hungarian master teachers. Also, what I saw was a unified curriculum, taught in every city, town, and village in Hungary. There was no competition. I therefore concluded that what I was seeing was Kodály's "method." Only some years later did I come to understand that Kodály's way of educating his nation's children musically could not be transplanted here—that to attempt to do so would be a grave mistake because of the diversity of our culture and the differences in our social structure. When I first realized that we would need many different versions of the Kodály "method" in our heterogeneous society, I was dismayed. Only slowly did I fathom that Kodály's philosophy, not a strict methodology, was the backbone of anything that might be developed in this country, and that we must therefore produce teachers who are competent, musically secure, independent, and imaginative enough to craft their own versions of "the method."

questions have now been answered in the affirmative, as is quite clear from the demand for Kodály-trained teachers nationwide and from videotapes of such teachers at work in inner-city classrooms. We know now that Kodály's ideas and his colleagues' teaching tools are effective in a great variety of settings and age groupings.

I expressed concern that the computer would one day control us if we did not learn to control it, and I suggested that the capacity to evaluate and discriminate, which is one of the benefits of Kodály training, would be an invaluable asset in a computer-dominated society. I spoke of America's need for the togetherness and group responsibility that has produced the Japanese economic miracle, and of the simultaneous need for individual attention so that problem children do not get lost in the crowd — opposites that the best Hungarian teachers handle so beautifully in the classroom.

I warned about going too fast and superficially, and I quoted Gunther Schuller, then president of New England Conservatory, as saying that although music was of course for all people, it was dangerous to broaden our efforts unless we also deepened them. I talked about the certainty of Kodály's ideas being attacked as lacking in creativity by our type of society. I said that Kodály expected creativity as a consequence of good teaching. Now I feel that we have fallen far short of the mark in this area; we have given the children musical tools with which to be creative, but rarely provided a model or shown ways to go about using the tools at their disposal. Our children do not, for the most part, explore, improvise, or compose. Hungarian teachers fall short in this respect too; however, I have seen two beautiful examples of creativity in the teaching of Klára Kokas and Klára Nemes right here this summer that cannot help but transfer itself to children.

In 1969 I felt that the two biggest problems in the way of adapting Kodály's ideas to another culture were a lack of proper materials and of adequate teacher training. The United States has by now made considerable progress in both directions. Not only have several good folk song collections appeared, but publishers of school music textbooks have recently begun to incorporate more and more folk songs rather than the often trashy music composed to fit a pedagogical concept. As for teacher training, several Kodály programs have developed at other universities, the earliest being KMTI, Holy Names, and Silver Lake College. Toward the end of my 1969 summer course speech I said it was my dream to establish a Kodály Center where we could start all over, from the bottom up, in preparing a music teacher. That dream became a reality in the fall of 1969, when the Kodály Musical Training Institute established the first such program. But KMTI was not without its problems over the years. The only way to establish and keep the standard Péter Erdei and I had set as a goal was to remain independent — in control of what was taught and who would teach it. Doing so has caused many financial problems, since we have not had at our disposal the resources of a large university — such as a good library, building facilities, a printing press, or a captive student body from which to draw enrollment. A central question for KCA, now that I will retire as its director,‡ is whether it should remain independent or try to become part of a larger institution.

Our Center's board of trustees has always looked to me for leadership in matters of academic policy and the issue of what kind of an institution KCA should be. Because someone else will ultimately have to be responsible and because I felt I should not make decisions for the future alone, Péter Erdei, when he visited KCA's 1988 summer course just a year ago, had the brilliant idea to invite an internationally respected group of Kodály-trained educators to discuss the situation in the context of the whole Kodály movement and the role KCA might play in its future development.* This committee has met twice in the past year and made recommenda-

---

‡Though in 1989 I planned soon to retire from the directorship of KCA, those plans were necessarily deferred. See chapter 6, "A Historical Perspective and a Look at the Future."

*Members of the Academic Advisory Committee for KCA's future were Péter Erdei, chairman; Jean Sinor; Annetta Miller, of Kenyatta University; Karen Kendrick; and Denise Bacon.

tions, but was careful to say it would be up to me and KCA's board to decide which recommendations to follow and how to implement them. The committee's recommendations are as follows:

1. That Kodály's philosophy, which is his greatest legacy, be understood as greater than music literacy as an end itself, on a worldwide basis.
2. That the Kecskemét experience become known and identified as a beacon light and the best model to follow, both in teacher training and classroom teaching.
3. That a model of excellence be available in every country where Kodály spreads, in both teacher training and classroom teaching.
4. That teachers who are struggling to learn, even if from mediocre models or inadequately trained teachers, be encouraged to seek the best and to improve themselves constantly, rather than be criticized for producing less than perfect results by those who are fortunate enough to have been close to the "authentic" source.
5. That we all learn from one another, that we try to understand and appreciate the adaptations of other countries. In this respect, it is important for every concerned teacher to join the International Kodály Society and to attend its conferences whenever possible, and to make the effort and sacrifice to study at Kecskemét, in either summer or academic-year courses, to expand one's knowledge and refresh one's spirit.
6. That we always keep in mind Kodály's goal of universal harmony and that we realize the power of music to create greater humanity and peace among us all.

Now, to consider KCA's part in this larger context just described: as I said twenty years ago in that 1969 Dana School of Music speech, I can tell you what I would like for the KCA of the future, but I cannot predict whether it will happen, or even whether my specific goals now are right for the long term.

First, I would like to see KCA become a western Kecskemét,

where excellence can be found both in teacher training and in classroom teaching, perhaps through our graduates in their own communities rather than at the Center's own model schools, since these are constantly changing. As anyone knows who has taught in inner-city Boston, where we have had programs in about twenty-five schools over the past nineteen years, continuity is impossible because Boston schools are always closing and the children moving to other schools. We now have a good possibility to develop a continuous model in a Boston suburb, if the school can survive financially.

Second, I would like to see KCA be a place that will benefit the whole Kodály movement — a place where people can get answers to their questions and help for their needs. This was one of the recommendations of the Academic Advisory Committee: that KCA develop a resource center that could help people not only in the United States but in other countries as well. We must find or invite knowledgeable people, such as Mihaly Ittzés or Katalin Komlós (and we must identify their American counterparts), to help in such areas as organizing and developing our library and collecting research in Kodály-related fields.

Third, I feel KCA should provide services to colleges, universities, and school systems wanting to hold Kodály seminars or develop Kodály programs or curricula.

Finally, KCA should expand its own publications and videotapes and also be a clearinghouse for Kodály-related materials and publications issued by other U.S. institutions. Students wishing to acquire a book published by KMTI, Holy Names, or Silver Lake College should know how it can be obtained by writing or phoning KCA. If someone from Australia wants to have Deanna Hoerman's books, or obtain information on her research efforts or on the latest developments there, that person should be able to find out where to get those things by contacting KCA's library. KCA should also occasionally sponsor good new publications of its own graduates and faculty or others having something of special interest to offer. Implementing these ideas will take time and money, however, and people will have to be willing to pay for both services and information.

On a more philosophical level, I would like to see KCA put emphasis on cultivating a heightened awareness and sensitivity in coming generations of both children and teachers. We must use music in such a way as to create, as envisioned by President Bush, a "kinder, gentler" world. This can happen only if children are nurtured in such a spirit from the beginning. Teachers graduating from universities and conservatories should be thinking, not that they want to teach only in the high school, but rather how they can use their knowledge where it counts most — with the very youngest children and, at the opposite end, with those who will become teachers. To work in the latter field, one must have superior knowledge, musical skills, dedication, and commitment on the level of a Péter Erdei and his faculty.

I hope that KCA will always keep a strong connection to Kecskemét, as long as its program remains under the leadership of a person with the kind of talent and commitment exhibited by Péter Erdei. I have already proposed to Péter a plan for expanded collaboration between our two institutions. Whether it materializes or not, the bond between us is strong, going back to before the Kecskemét Institute was founded, and I am confident that the collaboration will continue in some form. We cannot help but be stronger functioning together than separately.†

To sum up: my wish for the KCA of the future is that it will be a place that truly exemplifies Kodály's philosophy and spirit.

---

†The plan referred to was to offer a joint Kecskemét-KCA certificate for various summer course options: four summers divided between Kecskemét and KCA in any of three possible combinations, depending on students' finances for travel and tuition. Other special certificates were planned as well for conductors and performers. These plans never materialized, owing to the unexpected loss of KCA's headquarters and the subsequent transfer of its teacher-training program to Capital University.

6 Péter Erdei rehearsing Dana Hall School chapel choir, 1968.

7 The "pilot class" sings American folk songs on the stage of the Liszt Academy, Budapest, 1970.

8 Pilot class 1969–1970. Far left: Péter Erdei, Betsy Moll, Márta Nemesszeghy, Denise Bacon, Sarolta Kodály.

9 Prof. Erzsébet Szönyi teaching pilot class at Dana School of Music summer course, 1969. The two boys are David Samour and Louis Bergonzi; they now teach at the New England Conservatory and the East-man School of Music.

10 First Kecskemét summer seminar, 1970. Márta Nemesszeghy, Sr. Mary Alice Hein, Anna Hamvás, Sr. Lorna Zemke, Katalin Forrai, Denise Bacon, László Vikár.

11 Key players from the early years meet again at 1991 IKS Conference in Calgary. Left to right: Ann Patterson, Erzsébet Szönyi, Katalin Forrai, Betsy Moll, Lois Choksy, Denise Bacon.

12 Hungarian faculty learning *Little Sally Water,* 1971 KMTI summer course, Bridgeport. Clockwise from left: Denise Bacon, Erzsébet Hegyi, Kati Komlós, Helga Szabó ("Sally"), Maria Katanics, Klára Kokas.

13 Margaret Holden's choir from Blackpool, England, performed a concert at the first KMTI summer course, University of Bridgeport, Connecticut, 1971.

Part Two

The Kodály Philosophy

7. What the Kodály Concept Offers

This chapter is adapted from "Kodály for the Classroom Teacher," a speech given at Tennessee Technological University, Cookeville, Tennessee, in 1971.

WHAT IS THE KODALY CONCEPT?

The Kodály concept is a way of musical education that strives to achieve a synthesis of all the skills necessary to develop complete musicianship. It was inspired by and developed under the guidance of the famous Hungarian composer, philosopher, and educator Zoltán Kodály (1882–1967).

Kodály believed that music was necessary to the life of every human being and that no person could be a complete whole without the civilizing influence of great art. He also believed that music is not the property of the elite only, but that it should and can be accessible to every child. He felt that the soul of a child is sacred and that it must be fed only the best, pure, live art.

The Kodály concept is at least two important things: a philosophy affecting total education, and a unique course of sequential musical instruction — different in the hands of every teacher, as different as that teacher's training, interests, and imagination allow.

In his native Hungary, Kodály's efforts to create a renaissance of musical taste among the populace resulted in the widespread musical literacy of the present generation of youth. The average Hungarian child and young adult is able to read and write music as his own mother tongue, at a level from simple to very advanced, according to the plan under

[75]

which he learns (or has learned) — twice weekly or daily. Thus the young Hungarian has a priceless treasure that is his forever — the understanding and enjoyment of great music.

The teaching of music in the Kodály manner has led to other benefits for Hungarian children. The results of daily music in the core curriculum have made a remarkable impression on the educational field in general. Children's capacities for logical thinking, concentration, retention, and memory have been increased, thereby resulting in a better application and use of time in other studies.*

Further benefits in Hungary have been observed in the area of character and personality development. Because one of the basic tenets of the method is that a child shall always learn pleasurably (through games in the early stages) and that he should be refreshed in mind, body, and spirit as a result of his music lesson, there is a high degree of motivation to progress and to excel. Children trained in this manner develop a strong feeling of individual responsibility for the good of the whole group; shy and withdrawn children become involved as they discover the feeling of elation that comes with success. Success is assured because this way of teaching starts where a child is and goes from the known to the unknown. Conscious knowledge of concepts is abstracted only from material that is thoroughly familiar and that has been previously experienced unconsciously and practiced repeatedly. By the time a child consciously identifies a new concept, he is enormously pleased with his great discovery.

*While in Hungary in 1968, I wrote in a report on education there: "According to Dr. József Szarka, head of the Pedagogical Institute here, there are six areas in which a Hungarian must be educated. They are (1) the intellectual, (2) the moral or ethical, (3) the emotional, (4) the physical, (5) the aesthetic, and (6) the political. ... Among the reasons why music plays such an important part in the total curriculum here, Dr. Szarka said that music was the only subject that touched on every one of these six areas. ... The proportion of government funds for education spent on music reflects the attitude of the Hungarian government that music is a key subject, perhaps even the key subject in the school curriculum" ("Can We Afford to Ignore the Kodály Method?," *National Association of Independent Schools Bulletin*, December 1968).

WHAT IS UNIQUE IN KODALY?

The Kodály concept is a sequential pedagogy leading to musical literacy for any child with average musical aptitude, an objective it shares with many other methods. Except in rare cases and under unusual circumstances (such as under the tutelage of an especially gifted teacher), this objective has not been reached by any method in the United States or, to my knowledge, in other countries. But the musical literacy of the current generation of Hungarian youth has been a model and an incentive that has driven us to attempt an adaptation of Kodály's concepts here. Every U.S. pilot school that has thus far had the benefit of authentic Kodály instruction has achieved a level of musical literacy people have thought impossible.

The Kodály concept assumes that there is no such thing as an unmusical child and that any child may develop a high degree of musical literacy regardless of talent.

The process of children arriving at a conscious knowledge and understanding of masterworks of all cultures through the music of their own culture is a unique idea that comes directly from Kodály himself.

The concept is based on the human voice, an instrument that is free and accessible to every child, and is therefore probably the least expensive method of teaching music on a mass basis that now exists.

WHAT CAN THE KODALY CONCEPT GIVE OUR SOCIETY?

Most importantly, the Kodály concept holds something of permanent value for every child, regardless of race, creed, or talent. Secondly, it fosters values that our society badly needs: the ability to think logically and independently, to discriminate, to recognize and desire excellence. It trains a child to be more observant, to become more sensitive to those around him, and to develop his own abilities to his highest potential.

Tangibly, it can raise the level of musical taste and create an audience for the performing arts.† Through its use of folk song, it can bring the peoples of various ethnic backgrounds closer together and in so doing can create a greater appreciation for our own cultural heritage. If well taught, it can offer the possibility of success to even the most ungifted child. It can bring joy into the lives of average people, whose spirit can be lifted and ennobled by the contact with a mysterious force that is highly creative and personal, and that leaves a person different forever once it has touched him. It can help to create a more complete human being — one who is educated not only intellectually, but emotionally and aesthetically as well.

†"For culture, Kodály felt that three things were necessary: tradition, taste, and spiritual integrity. The means to this end were achieved through relative solmization, folk song (as the cornerstone of musical value), and singing" ("The Kodály Philosophy: Can It Make a Difference?," KMTI Summer Course Opening Address, July 1, 1974).

8. Kodály's Message: Unsuspected Gold

This chapter is adapted from a paper read at the Organization of American Kodály Educators (OAKE) Conference, Seattle, Washington, March 12, 1983.

As a result of the development of both our national and the international Kodály movements over the past fifteen years, and with the Kodály Centennial celebrations behind us, we need to assess the current state of things and deal with the question raised at last year's Boston University KCA Centennial Celebration: "Where do we go from here — what comes next?"* Though a great deal of progress has been made in the Kodály movement, and many new paths have been opened up in the whole field of music education, it is recognized increasingly that, in this daily expanding technological and computerized society, man cannot live by bread alone. We need the other side of the coin badly — the satisfaction of our deeper, human instincts, the feeding not only of the stomach but of the spirit.

I don't believe even those of us who have considerable experience in this movement are fully taking advantage of Kodály's message, let alone those who have only recently been introduced to it or are just becoming aware of it. For instance, I am deeply disturbed that teachers and students are too often concerned with whether one should call a triplet rhythmic figure *tripleti, triola,* or *ti-ti-ti* instead of with

*I addressed these questions in two speeches during the centennial year: "Where Do We Go From Here?" (1982 KCA academic year opening address) and "Reflections on Zoltán Kodály's Centennial" (speech for Kodály Centennial at Boston University, November 12, 1982).

what Kodály had to say about the need for a teacher to become both a complete musician and complete human being. If we do understand the message, we are certainly not getting it across sufficiently to overcome the objections of, and the damage done by, those who misinterpret and misuse it. If we *were* getting that message across, we would not have the difficulties we do in trying to persuade authorities of the value of music in the core curriculum and those of us with organized Kodály programs would not have such difficulty in getting financial support for them.

What is Kodály's message to us and what is most important about that message? Is it that at last we have a system that will teach music literacy, that at last we have an alternative to college students' suffering through boring theory courses that do not teach them how to take down even a simple melody in dictation? Is it that finally we have a sure-fire way to interest even the most recalcitrant kids in music and a way to help children who might otherwise be termed hopeless monotones? Is it that finally we have found a way to make order out of the jungle of rhythmic, melodic, and formal elements that traditionally have been regarded as the incomprehensible stuff and unfathomable mystique of music?

It is all these things, but it is much more. Those great men and women who have contributed memorably to the progress of the human race have usually been visionaries, searching for truth, beauty, and meaning — looking for answers beyond the known, seeking to expand the limits of human horizons. Kodály was one of these. We are all looking for those answers, but we lack the force and power of a Kodály.

Kodály sought the enrichment of life and development of human potential through the medium of music, and he had an all-encompassing vision and concern for humanity at large. He believed these intangibles to be the birthright and property of everyone, not merely those talented in the field of music. Kodály was interested not only in music — he loved literature, poetry, drama, art, sculpture, and nature. He spoke many languages and was particularly interested in the marriage of text and melody. He was equally at home with the high art of royalty and the folk art of peasants, and he met both learned scholars and children on their own terms.

One of the false ideas that have emerged from the Kodály experience in this country is the rigidity ascribed to it by uninformed music educators. Kodály was anything but rigid, except where standard was concerned — a better word might have been *uncompromising.*

The versatility and universality of Kodály's philosophy suggest that there are riches inherent in that philosophy as yet unexplored. The current practical applications of that philosophy are merely the tip of the iceberg. Kodály's ideas have applicability to a great variety of situations and allow for great freedom of interpretation. We hear constantly that colleges and universities do not want to restrict themselves to a Kodály approach — that they want to take a more eclectic approach in their music education programs. The truth and the irony are that Kodály was one of the greatest eclectics music education has ever known. He traveled to many countries, studied many systems, concepts, and methods of music education, and ended up taking what he thought was best from several of them.

The music curriculum that gradually evolved in Hungary, eventually resulting in an almost universally literate generation of Hungarians, and attracting worldwide attention at the 1964 ISME Conference in Budapest, was not even Kodály's doing, but that of his colleagues — most notably Jenö Ádám. But none of what we have today in the Kodály movement would have happened without that inspiration, genius, and force of personality for which Kodály is remembered by his colleagues and students.

László Eösze, author of *Kodály: His Life and Work* (Boston: Crescendo, 1982), writes of Kodály having accomplished singlehandedly a prodigious, threefold task as composer, musicologist, and teacher. What did Kodály keep trying to impress on his colleagues and students? What was his message to them, which has become our legacy? Certainly not *ta ti-ti ta,* See-saw, or "preparation, presentation, and practice." The answer lies in his compositions, his contributions to the various aspects of folklore, and the philosophy expressed in his *Selected Writings.*

Why his compositions, you may ask? What do they have to do with his message, or with us as teachers? They *were* his message. One knows a man best by his works, his deeds, his output — in Kodály's case, by his compositions. They reflect his deepest concerns, aspirations, and hopes for his country. Kodály wrote about nature (*Mátra Pictures, Mountain Nights, Summer Evening*), about freedom (*Hymn to Zrinyi, Peacock Variations*), about patriotism (*Psalmus Hungaricus*); his compositions expressed human emotions all the way from sorrow (*I Will Go Look for Death*), compassion (*The Aged*), and anger (*Jesus and the Traders*) to joy and exaltation (*Te Deum* and *Hymn to Saint Stephen*). In the compositions he wrote for children can be found not only the exercises that were to lead them to musical literacy but songs encompassing a wide range of interests and emotions, from the lively *Dancing Song* and the humorous *Hippity-Hoppity* (a nonsense song) to the religious feeling expressed in *Ave Maria* — emotions that need to be felt and expressed by children the world over.

Kodály's gift to his own countrymen through his lifelong research into Hungary's folk culture not only preserved a priceless and permanent cultural heritage but also pointed the way for other countries and has had a lasting impact on them. In America, before Kodály spoke at Stanford University in 1966, folk music was the province of anthropologists only and had little to do with music education, nor were its links to art music understood. In Germany, the evolving Orff movement was totally unaware of folk music in the early 1960s, yet look at the use of folk music in Orff curriculum today! Compare the series songbooks of the 1960s with those of today; nearly every good series contains a wealth of folk music seldom encountered two decades ago. Not only that, but Kodály's idea that one starts with the folk music of one's own mother tongue and proceeds to that of neighboring and ultimately faraway countries has been expanded in our nation's music curricula by the inclusion of folk music of many cultures. And we have not even begun to tap the resources available to us for creating better communication among the earth's peoples through the medium of music.

We have been richly blessed through Kodály's legacy as composer and musicologist, but as teachers ourselves, probably most blessed by his ideas as a *teacher* — not so much as a teacher of composition in the Liszt Academy or a teacher of children in schools (which latter he was not), but in a larger sense — as a leader of musical reforms intended to raise the whole level of musical life, both as far as professional musicians and children in the schools were concerned. This part of Kodály's message is the most valuable, and we have not yet thoroughly grasped it.

Kodály continually tried to educate his students in the Liszt Academy and teachers who came to him for advice, through articles, speeches, and visits to the schools. The things he had to say apply to all who want to study, teach, perform, or create music — they are universally true and are not intended merely for so-called Kodály educators. It would be far better if we did not have to refer to the Kodály method, concept, system, or approach. There really is no such thing, for what Kodály wanted was only what every good performer or music teacher wants, even those who believe only in fixed do and totally reject the idea of relative solfege. Why then, are these things, which everyone considers valuable and wants, particularly associated with Kodály? Mainly, I think, because these principles were proven true and had an astonishing result in Kodály's own country — a result that has not been found to date in any other country.

What are some of these common threads we can all believe in? There may be many more, but the following come to mind immediately:

Music belongs to everyone.

Man is incomplete without music.

One should begin as early as possible (according to Kodály, even before the child is born).

Teachers should be complete musicians; namely (according to Schumann's ideas as summarized by Kodály), have educated ears, minds, hearts, and hands.

Only the best, most valuable music should be used (beginning, according to Kodály, with the music of one's own ethnic heritage).

Order, sequence, and process are important in creating musical literacy and understanding.

Music must be taught so that it is a joyous experience for children.

Because Kodály was committed to the idea that a good music education was the birthright of everyone (not only the talented or privileged) and because of his force of character and personality as a leader, he was able to prove that such education:

1. Was for the youngest infant to the adult amateur. Background, talent, and experience did not matter.
2. Was for the sophisticated urban children of professional parents in Budapest or for children of peasants in the tiniest rural villages.
3. Was for the gifted Liszt Academy student planning a concert career or the nursery-kindergarten teacher.
4. Was for those who had normal home lives and advantages as well as the children of state orphanages, for those of high I.Q. as well as the learning disabled.
5. Was for both those who could or could not sing or play an instrument.

Here in America, we are still thinking about *ta ta ti-ti ta* when we should be thinking of bringing the benefits of music teaching such as that inspired by the Kodály philosophy to a wider variety of audiences, for instance:

1. To day-care centers, nursery schools, and private classes in parents' own living rooms (here I refer to teachers whose school careers are temporarily disrupted in order to raise their own children)
2. To high school elective courses
3. To junior and senior church choirs, and to children's and adult community choirs
4. To special schools such as those that have Montessori or Waldorf programs or that serve disabled and emotionally disturbed children
5. To community music schools for children and adult amateurs
6. To bands and orchestras in both public and private schools
7. To retirement homes and senior citizens' groups
8. To parent volunteers and other adults

So far, Kodály-inspired music education has been largely the province of elementary education; it has had limited success in a few college courses, mainly for the training of elementary school teachers rather than for the benefit of future performers. It has been introduced into a small number of church choirs, but by and large, the prestigious American Choral Directors Association and the American Guild of Organists have not become interested in it; it is beginning to be tolerated by band directors, largely through the pioneering efforts of Jerry Jaccard. One of our young students from Mexico recently started a senior citizens' program in her country, the response from which so moved and inspired her that she wants to commit the rest of her life to bringing music to the aged.

There are unexplored fields where a hidden pot of gold may be found that will be a blessing — if not to the pocketbook, then at least to the spirit. Although the Kodály philosophy holds potential for such a wide variety of situations, it is certainly not a panacea for everything that ails music education. Nevertheless, it can be a constant underpinning, a source of inspiration and hope for us all, because its tenets came from the mind of a genius who made his ideas work for the benefit of an entire culture. Kodály's eclecticism needs to be recognized. His philosophy of music and general education is applicable to the mainstream of life. László Eösze wrote that "Kodály's art is still alive and is still of universal value, because he undertook to express the truth of his people and his period." [1] Let us seek diligently to understand that truth, and labor to adapt it in the spirit of our people, in the context of *American* society, in our time.

[1] László Eösze, *Zoltán Kodály: His Life in Pictures* (Budapest: Corvina Press, 1971).

9. The Practicality and Applicability of Kodály's Philosophy

This chapter is excerpted from a speech delivered at the Maine Music Educators Association Conference, May 17, 1985.

Recently, a doctoral candidate at a university in Iowa wrote to me for information on research studies that would support the subject of his thesis, which was to be an attempt to prove the superiority of the Kodály concept of music education over other methods. I was horrified, as I don't believe in the superiority of one method over another. Any method or concept is only as good as the teacher teaching it; if a teacher is a good musician, uses good material, is logical and creative in using it, and loves to teach, he or she will be successful no matter which approach is used, whether Orff, Suzuki, Dalcroze, traditional, or other.

Kodály himself maintained that the sequencing which is a hallmark of Kodály-based programs is only a skeleton on which a gifted and imaginative teacher may hang his or her ideas. A recent graduate who is now developing a Kodály program in a community center after-school program for inner-city children came to the discovery, in a very short time, that the pedagogical sequence she had learned and taught under KCA supervision in our practice-teaching school was not adequate for children who, though they had the same background, were in a different setting. Because the needs of the children were foremost in her mind, and because she was well aware of Kodály's overall philosophical principles, she felt secure in experimenting with her own ideas. She kept in mind, above all, Kodály's belief that the children must have a pleasurable experience and must not look on music class as a tedious or boring experience. She plans their lessons so as to alternate periods of concentration and relaxation, and she constantly challenges the children to succeed individually, discarding or rearranging what did not work from her previous experience. After six months, she is finally getting a handle on this difficult teaching environment; doing so has increased her own self-confidence and feeling of worth immeasurably.

The applicability of Kodály's philosophy is enormous, because there need be no restrictions on it and because it is practical in many diverse situations. The basic tenets of Kodály's philosophy and even some of the system's specific techniques have relevance for persons in all areas of music education, whether they are general teachers, performers, church choir directors, or band or orchestra leaders, and the same tenets have significance for people at all age levels from preschool through teacher training.

The common notion that Kodály is only for the elementary classroom is patently false. The process used at the Liszt Academy level is the same as that used in first grade; the materials and the time needed to master a concept are different at these opposite age levels, but the process is the same, and it is therefore possible for a college professor to learn from the first-grade curriculum.

None of us can get along in this world without the ability to read and write and to use the language. Our language is music, and we all want to understand, master, and use it well. Language is an ability that constantly grows as we study and use it. A child does not stop learning the English language once the alphabet has been learned or some fluency in the reading process acquired. If children have had good grounding in grammar, they will have been given the tools with which to write themselves; if they have read or have had fairy tales read to them when very young, their imagination will have been stimulated to create stories of their own; if they have been pleasurably introduced to childhood classics, they will want to read more and more literature as adults; if they have been involved in a good dramatic production they will doubtless become avid theatergoers. They may even become interested in learning other languages.

The process in music is similar. Kodály believed that music as a language had the power to develop human potential, and also that, as Schumann said, "There is no end to learning." This, for a teacher of any kind of music, is one of the most hopeful statements ever made. Too often, music teachers never attend concerts, refresher workshops, or advanced music courses once the precious B.M. degree is in their hands, because they know that, in many cases, they are being hired more for baby-sitting than for teaching purposes, or they feel instinctively that no one will care whether they produce beautiful results or whether they constantly strive to better themselves — it doesn't really matter so long as the class is under control and causes no problem. As for band, chorus, and orchestra leaders, too often their greatest value appears to be in cementing good public relations, as produced by performances parents or school systems can be proud of, rather than in what the children actually learn from their musical experience.

These conditions are not true in enlightened school systems or communities, but are general enough to discourage many in the music profession from remaining in it or prospective candidates from entering it.

How does the Kodály philosophy address such problems? One of the ways is in saying: You, the teacher, count! You are important. Your own musical development, your self-respect, your achievements are important — if not to your superiors, then to you yourself, and to the children and adults you teach. You cannot motivate children if you are not motivated yourself. You can't teach children to love music if you don't love it yourself. But to love music, one must know it. Therefore, one must make oneself into the best musician possible.

Kodály believed that students and teachers should be in competition with themselves, not with each other. Thus I have seen the best Hungarian teachers (there are also bad ones!) single out for help the most problematic child in the class. Things are always done in group activity first; when the group as a whole is reasonably secure, an individual child (whom the teacher feels is likely to be successful) is picked to demonstrate individually. The success of such a child motivates other children to want the same success, and eventually the most shy or fearful child in the class cannot resist the challenge. Children are never laughed at when they fail to answer correctly. Kodály himself, interacting with his students at the Liszt Academy (where he taught folk music and composition) rarely praised them, but he always challenged them individually.

Kodály's philosophy says that only excellence will do. Give a child only the best possible music; stay close to beautiful music, immerse yourself in it; participate in music making; go to concerts; listen to masterpieces; open your mind; look into all aspects of life; study art and science too. Kodály quotes that great pianist and pedagogue of by-gone years Theodor Leschetizky, "Keine Kunst ohne Leben, Keine Leben ohne Kunst" (There is no art without life, no life without art). [1]

When I took my first steps to bring the authentic Kodály concept to this country in 1968 (Mary Helen Richards had preceded me, but her adaptation was only a taste, admittedly planned for classroom teachers rather than music specialists), I had no idea of what I was starting or getting into. I wanted to see some changes in American music education, but my immediate goal was merely to produce some kind of model others could see. The difficulties over the past fifteen years have been enormous, and we are still trying to produce the kind of model I know is possible in this country; nevertheless, in spite of obstacles, the rewards have been great, for the Kodály movement *has* made an impact. If not, why is there now a national Kodály society — OAKE (Organization of American Kodály Educators)? Why are over thirty countries represented in the International Kodály Society membership? Why are performers, administrators, whole school systems, colleges, community day-care centers, therapists, special-education teachers, psychologists, preschool personnel, and parents interested in it?

It is because Kodály's philosophy is a universal one, espoused by all great thinkers in every field. It reaches beyond music. Kodály's philosophy is well expressed in his *Selected Writings*. "Real art is one of the most powerful forces in the rise of mankind, and he who renders it accessible to as many people as possible is a benefactor of humanity." [2] Also: "It is our firm conviction that mankind will live the happier when it has learnt to live with music more worthily. Whoever works to promote this end, in one way or another, has not lived in vain." [3] Lastly, and with this one I throw out to you the challenge of the Kodály philosophy: "It is much more important who the singing master at Kisvárda is than who the director of the Opera House is, because a poor director will fail. . . . But a bad teacher may kill off the love of music for thirty years from thirty classes of pupils." [4]

The Kodály approach to music education offers us a way — not the only way, but a good one — to avoid this kind of tragedy and to bring about that condition Kodály spoke of "when all people in all lands are brought together through singing, and when there is a universal harmony." [5]

[1] Zoltán Kodály, *Selected Writings* (Budapest: Corvina Press, 1974), p. 192.

[2] Ibid., p. 199.

[3] Ibid., p. 206.

[4] Ibid., p. 124.

[5] Ibid., p. 215.

10. Bridging the Gap: Kodály the Educator and Kodály the Composer

This chapter first appeared in somewhat different form in the KCA Newsletter, June 1992.

When music educators first become exposed to the Kodály concept, their initial fascination is, lamentably, not with the rich wellspring of Kodály's compositional output — much of it written to help children acquire musical literacy, understanding, and taste — but rather with the pedagogical techniques developed by his colleagues. As a result, Kodály is far better known in this country as an educator than as a composer.

Bartók's and Kodály's work together in the field of folk music is well known to most American music educators; Bartók's compositions are also well known here because he came to this country permanently when the Nazis took over Hungary. Kodály, on the other hand, remained in Hungary and directed his compositional talent to producing works that would raise the standard of musical taste in his own country, to lift the Hungarian national spirit from what he described as its "present primitive state of musical comprehension."

When Americans first observed the remarkable results of Kodály's fifty-year efforts and the astonishing degree of musical literacy they found in Hungarian youth, they naturally wanted the same for American children. Capitalizing on Kodály's lifelong efforts, many American music educators sought training in the Kodály system and over the past twenty-five years have created a revolution of their own in musical standards and tastes. But for the most part, their knowledge of Kodály's compositions is limited to the easier pieces their children's choirs are able to perform — and even so, these beautiful works are not widely known or performed by either Kodály-trained or traditional music teachers. Mrs. Zoltán Kodály has often answered those who have asked her what her husband was like as a person by saying, "If you want to know my husband, you must know his music."

I have long lamented the distance between performing artists and educators and wanted to bring them into a closer appreciation of the contributions that each can make toward creating a musically literate, aware, and appreciative society. I have shared Kodály's concern, expressed several decades ago, that there would be no one to listen to the works of new young composers in fifty years' time if children were not brought up to be musically literate. Not only has that time arrived for contemporary composers, but now even the great masters are increasingly relegated to relative oblivion by the apathy of a public whose senses have been dulled by the second-rate pap to which they as children were subjected in their most formative years through most school music programs.

Educators, performers, and composers need to work together to awaken interest in and love for high-quality music of both past and present. Zoltán Kodály showed a way in Hungary that has borne fruit all over the world. To accomplish this goal he largely sacrificed his career in composition. The world both lost and gained by this choice. His music must at last come into its own. Those who espouse the Kodály philosophy must finally recognize that his works are as important as his ideas and that there is a wealth of beauty and inspiration to be found in them. Let us hope that more and more children's choirs, church choirs, and amateur groups will perform them, for they contain messages of universal human truth and value.

11. Survival for Innovative Trends in Music Education

This chapter is adapted from a speech delivered on KCA Day, March 24, 1979.

Survival is a strong word, fraught with desperate connotations. Today as we look on this world, our first concern is physical survival. Pollution, nuclear war, genetic engineering — all are threats to human life. But these somehow seem distant problems in comparison to the necessity for financial survival, or job security and our daily bread and butter. Last on our list, but probably most important to each of us personally, is *spiritual* survival — the survival of value systems upon which a meaningful existence depends.

The art of music and the field of music education are in very real crisis; the state of performing musicians and teachers is equally deplorable — we are all in the same boat. California's Proposition 13 has accelerated the already severe budget-cutting process in all fields of education, with particularly strong axing in the arts. Innovative trends of promise such as Kodály, Orff, and Suzuki cannot afford to sit back complacently and say, "Oh, but we are different. Only excellence is going to survive and we are excellent. We are somehow better than traditional music education and so we have a better chance." Such blindness can only lead to our eventual demise.

Schools have traditionally been resistant to educational change and aesthetic concerns; furthermore, our society basically thinks, acts, and does as it pleases. Anything goes, so long as it does not rock the boat too badly. We overlook the deadly boredom our educational system produces (for the most part) and see nothing morally corrupt in educating for skills, credentials, and economic security alone.

All this has been going on for quite some time — long enough that only revolutionary action can change it.

Perhaps the collapse of the overall educational system would not be too great a tragedy. From the ashes might arise an edifice dedicated to a lifelong learning experience rather than lip service to a facsimile of learning, the blueprint for which is drawn mainly to conform to a prescribed set of courses and experiences with predictable results in terms of grades: A equals success, C– or less equals failure.

Music education hasn't too far to fall in the educational process, since it has never really been considered an important part of education. We are normally conditioned by our parents, our early education, and our environment. We have been taught that music is a genteel art for female accomplishment, that it is entertainment, or, in the educational process, that it has public relations value. We have not been taught that it is an important tool of communication, a means of emotional enrichment, personal expression, intellectual balance, and creative fulfillment. Those of us who are teachers may personally have observed these benefits, but what have we done to assure that others know of and experience them?

Music educators themselves must accept the responsibility for the role assigned to music in the educational process, and for the current dearth of music jobs in the overall education market. The quality of much music instruction has been of so little value as to invite axing, and we have not created either the demand or the audience for music as an art.

Into this already declining atmosphere came the Orff, Kodály, and Suzuki concepts with an immediately revitalizing effect educationally. Although these concepts have made an impact, they have also created controversy and come under sharp attack. Why? Probably because they have challenged the status quo and have strengthened weak points or supplied the missing links to a complete musical experience. They have gone a long way toward solving some of the problems for which our traditional music education has been seeking answers for decades. The Kodály concept has made great strides in musical literacy and has brought children everywhere into a closer awareness and understanding of their own cultural heritage. The Orff concept has turned children on, motivated them toward learning, and developed the latent creativity of children at all levels, from the most limited to the most gifted. The Suzuki concept has produced a high level of technical skill, excellence in performance, and a taste for high-quality music, all with average children; in fact, it has proved one of the most important tenets of the Kodály philosophy — that great music is not the property of the elite, talented, or privileged, but is accessible to everyone.

This latter point is one that all of music education would like to espouse but does not carry out in practice — mostly, I believe, because the average music educator cannot or does not know how to make this come true for every child under his or her tutelage. After all, here is a pretty strong claim — that a valid, meaningful, excellent, and complete musical experience is possible and is (or should be) available to every child. Music in the United States has been for an elite, those gifted enough to get into performing groups — the band, orchestra, or select chorus, and the final motivation has been performance at the district, all-state, regional, or national music conferences; or in private schools, performing at the Christmas or spring concerts or in the local and regional independent school orchestra and choral festivals. But three-fourths of those who are supposed to be studying music as a part of their total educational experience are told they are not good enough — they are told to keep quiet and "mouth the words but don't sing out loud" for fear of spoiling the concert. And what happens to the lucky one-fourth who made it into the performing group? Where are they twenty years and four children later? The motivation has disappeared — there is no longer an all-state concert to compete for. And what about the truly talented individual — the one who always got the solo part, the star performer who went on to become someone in the musical world? He or she is either set on a pedestal as an untouchable genius or regarded as a misfit who does not belong with normal people — unless, of course, he or she happened to make it big in the pop entertainment field.

There are rumblings in the music education profession now and attempts to change all this as educators realize they are perpetrating their own doomsday. Suddenly, music must be for every child. But how to service such an enormous and diverse population? The answer has been the eclectic approach. Take a little from here, a little from there, and stir it all up till you have a homogenized mess of nothing. A child should be musically literate, so give him or her flash cards and a few hand signals; he must be creative, so let him experiment with tape recorders or unorganized sound from any source he can imagine; he must perform, so let him bang on pots, pans, or Orff instruments; above all, he lives in a modern, pluralistic society, exposed to constant TV, and therefore he must have a balanced diet of Bach, Beethoven, Brahms, the folk songs of at least one hundred countries, rock, pop, electronic, aleatory, and anti-music, all thrown together in a free creative chaos. In this way, we should be able to create a nice balanced child with nice balanced emotions and nicely balanced tastes.

In my opinion, the current wave of eclecticism in music education is producing homogenized mediocrity and mass confusion. But we cannot stem the tide of a pluralistic society with excellence in any one area, whether it is Kodály, Orff, Suzuki, or any other system that we know to be excellent in itself. How are we who truly believe in what we are doing and know we have something good to offer going to survive, and how can we help the situation?

First of all, the proponents of differing methods, concepts, or systems — or of ideas within the same system — must stop being so competitive and defensive. One of the most characteristic aspects of the American value system is competition, which is unfortunately not always a productive kind of competition. In most fields of endeavor (and music education is no exception), we are concerned less with the kind of competition that tries to produce the highest quality possible than with competition that says, "My way is better than yours."

The minute we say, "My way is better than yours," or, "My way is best; therefore you should do it my way," we cut off all our options, and we also become a threat to established forces, thereby creating greater problems for ourselves.

We must stop thinking that we are all things to all people, that as proponents of whatever individual concept we espouse we have all the answers. Although we may inwardly be convinced that what we have to offer is best, we need to remember the adage "you can lead a horse to water, but you cannot make him drink." We have no right to claim that our own preference — whether it is Kodály, Orff, Dalcroze, Suzuki, or whatever — is better than other ways; such systems are no better than the teacher who uses them, and heaven only knows, all such concepts have imitators who are poorly trained, using only the gimmicks and making a travesty of the original ideas, thus seeming to disprove their concept's claim to excellence. At the same time, we should recognize that great minds are apt to run along the same track and that in many cases, innovative ideas are only educational philosophies that have been presented before but are rediscovered in a new light. In the case of the Kodály concept, there is little that is really new or innovative. Kodály's basic educational ideas are close to those of Piaget and other fine educators, and his musical tools and materials — the human voice, solmization, hand signs, folk and art music — have been used for hundreds of years by other methods. But Kodály pedagogy presents these familiar tools and materials in a fresh way and provides a sequence that can be highly flexible according to any given learning environment — a sequence that is pleasurable and that produces results (at least when the teacher has had good training and has good communicative skills). In short, the Kodály way works. But this is no reason for Kodály enthusiasts to force what is called the "Kodály method" down people's throats and tout it as a panacea for every musical ill that besets us.

To be effective, to help, and, yes, to survive, we must think of what we can *give* to music education, not what we can *impose* on it. Skills are not all that count; neither is "having fun in the classroom." We need to define our goals more clearly, and we must know what our own unique contributions are without trying to apply them to the whole of humanity. We need to recognize our similarities and differences, to capitalize on the possibilities of collaboration and co-operation, and to stop denigrating others' ideas where they are different.

Michael Palotai, who wrote the scathing article "Has Hungary Outgrown Kodály?," which I answered in a long rebuttal article in the September 1978 issue of the *Music Educators Journal*, rebutted my rebuttal in the March 1979 issue.* Among other things, he claims that I have not spelled out how intelligent amateurs or intelligent music lovers should be educated. He is right — I have not, nor do I intend to, because there are many good ways to educate amateurs and music lovers. I could not in good conscience claim that Kodály is the only or even best way to do this. For me personally, it is the most appealing and satisfying way, because I am myself and not someone else. Indeed, I once wrote an article on what my idea of good teacher training is, but it did not claim that the Kodály way is the only way to achieve it. Still, those of us who are attracted to the Kodály concept had better know why it is good, what it can offer, and how we intend to make it work.

Many methods are viable, good, and powerful in their own right, but when poorly trained or insecure teachers take little fragments from here and there and make compromises here and there, they water down the result. There are exceptions to this complaint, and I am not referring to the gifted, well-trained teacher who has taken the trouble to learn a variety of approaches, is a good musician, and has come up with an imaginative synthesis that is his or her own — that is an ideal way. But individual concepts such as Kodály, Orff, Dalcroze, and Suzuki are rarely allowed to succeed on

*Mr. Palotai's article appeared in the February 1978 issue of *Music Educators Journal*. My rebuttal ("Hungary Will Never Outgrow Kodály," *MEJ*, September 1978) pointed out the fallacy of criticizing the Kodály "method" when in fact no such thing exists. Much of his criticism pertained to the shortcomings of the weakest teachers (who can be found in Hungary, as anywhere) and to the rigidity of a highly centralized state educational system, which has little relevance to music educators in the United States.

their own terms. We can succeed best if we keep our minds on producing excellence in our own fields and encouraging others to do the same.

We would be foolish to ignore that we are a pluralistic society, but do we represent diversity in it, or only confusion? My goal is to lead the children, teachers, and laymen with whom I work to have a lifelong love affair with music. We must hold on to excellence at all costs, but we must also allow our colleagues to hold on to it. Nothing prevents us from borrowing from each other, from sharing, from coming up with something that veers away from a traditional Kodály, Orff, Suzuki, or whatever line, but each individual must be certain that the departure represents his or her best efforts. If there are enough good examples to choose from, we will simultaneously have coped with the problem of pluralism and of raising taste, or, if you will, of lessening this "homogenized mediocrity." But no one method, system, or concept can do it alone. We need good alternatives, to which people of different backgrounds, lifestyles, and tastes can relate. We must not look down on the child whose parents never knew anything but bebop and who wishes to learn a rock tune through hand signals and play it on a sousaphone or harmonica. Kodály said that the inherited inclinations of individuals must be the starting point. We do not have to teach a pop tune on a tonette if we don't want to, just because the child says he wants it. However, there may be teachers who feel it is a great challenge to teach a child to sing or play a pop tune on a harmonica, Orff instrument, or string bass, and there are certainly children for whom this represents achievement, self-expression, and very real pleasure. The point is that if people have enough *good* possibilities to choose from, they may, with sufficient exposure and the passage of time, eventually be able not only to distinguish but actually to come to like the valuable, rather than the trivial.

Music is one of the greatest, safest, and most rewarding means of communication. It is especially important to recognize and capitalize on this truth, in an age where either inability or unwillingness to communicate has caused many of our most severe problems. The Kodály concept fosters individual excellence within a framework of strong togetherness. We can and must be a powerful part of the educational process, and not just the music education process. But to achieve this we must work together with teachers of other concepts in a noncompetitive spirit — realizing, without fragmenting our potential contributions, that the whole is greater than the sum of its parts. Above all, we must not set art — in our case, the art of music — apart from daily life, for as Kodály said, "Powerful sources of spiritual enrichment spring from music. We must spare no effort to have them opened for as many people as possible." [1]

[1] Zoltán Kodály, *Selected Writings* (Budapest: Corvina Press, 1974), p. 126.

12. Kodály in the 1980s

This chapter is adapted from "Kodály in Context of the Eighties," a speech given at the Kodály Center of America's annual open house, March 21, 1981. Portions of the speech were published in the Midwest Kodály Music Educators Association Bulletin, July 1982.

It seems impossible that only ten short years ago the name of Kodály as an educator was barely known in this country, and that twenty years ago he was relatively unknown even as a composer. I thought his music daring and was quite shocked by a performance of *The Angels and the Shepherds* at a Christmas concert by the Glee Club at Dana Hall, where I was at the time the head of the music department. I thought the harmonies were too modern and difficult for those academically talented but, for the most part, musically illiterate girls to learn.

A generation has now passed since I first heard of Kodály, and though the curtain has fallen on the first act, the play has just begun. The groundwork has been laid and chief characters introduced, and enough has been accomplished to attract the attention and interest of a large audience. But what lies ahead? Will the play reach a satisfying climax or will it deflate in a disappointing dénouement? Will it be good enough to be absorbed into the permanent repertoire, to be adapted for other media?

I suspect no one would venture to predict or prophesy on these points. A year or so ago I remarked that we were now embarking on a second phase of the Kodály movement in this country. The first phase (during the 1970s) was one of wobbly experimentation in a new world, where the child takes its first faltering steps, again and again returning to the safety of its mother's arms; thus our early beginnings were strongly tied to Hungarian roots. We have experienced both the pleasures and pangs of childhood as the excitement of discovery has shaped and molded our new musical personalities — for there is no denying that all those who have seriously investigated the Kodály philosophy have in effect been "born again."

But danger lies ahead, similar to that for those who are born again in the original sense of the term. Many of us have rushed to latch on to this wonderful new concept, to join the bandwagon. Many of us feel we have been "born again," but for how many who have been "converted" will the experience of the Kodály movement remain a deep, life-enriching, transforming experience? That depends on two significant factors, without which no movement of such scope and potential as the Kodály concept can develop successfully — namely, the foresight and wisdom of its leaders and the quality and commitment of those who elect to follow it.

Americans are easily swayed by newness in everything from detergents to hairstyles, from clothes fashions to educational fads. It is not so much the thing itself that attracts them as the newness of it. But the newness soon wears off and the exciting new product, style, or idea soon becomes relegated to the dustbin of history. It could happen to the Kodály concept. If an idea or movement develops too fast or superficially, if the product is watered down too drastically, it will create its own demise; in the case of the Kodály concept, it could become diffused in that stream of homogenized mediocrity of which I am consistently complaining and which appears to be the mainstream of American music education. Let me give you an example. Lois Choksy's new book, *The Kodály Context* (Englewood Cliffs, N.J.: Prentice-Hall, 1981), gives an excellent synopsis of the Kodály philosophy and why we must let it guide our efforts, rather than just taking off with hand signals, do-re-mi, and ta ti-ti ta, and calling it Kodály. The book is comprehensive, offering suggestions on how to approach certain problems and giving a considerable amount of musical material; it will create a tremendous demand, and there will inevitably be a rash of Kodály courses developing in universities and colleges as a result. While the spread of the Kodály concept is certainly a desirable thing, to avoid the ultimate bursting of the bubble we must support such serious and important contributions as Choksy's book by providing in-depth opportunities for high-quality teacher training.

One cannot learn how to use Kodály's philosophical or musical ideas from a book alone; they must be observed, studied, and practiced under the tutelage of someone who has adapted them successfully from the original source and has become a model good enough for others to learn from. One can begin from a book, but one cannot ultimately achieve or contribute to the further progress of humankind from that base alone.

In only a handful of places in both the United States and Canada can one get the truly synthesized training that makes the difference between good and bad Kodály teaching. And even those institutions must tailor their offerings to the existing curricula of their music departments while facing the inevitable budget constraints and lack of acceptance by already entrenched musical forces. We must be grateful that there are a few such institutions where one can get high-quality training — their existence represents a considerable achievement and much hard work on the part of a few visionary people over the past decade. But for the Kodály concept to survive in the 1980s we must not only support and strengthen all of these existing institutions but also, in order to meet increased demand, encourage the development of Kodály programs in other institutions and under conditions that will allow for high-quality training.

What can we do, what must we do, to ensure survival? First, we must face the fact that we are not talking merely about the survival of the Kodály concept — we are facing the near extinction of music in the educational process. Unthinkable? Not at all, in the minds of politicians, administrators, school superintendents, school committees, and a large segment of the public. If we want music to survive in our society — and let us go one step further than the educational process, to the role our great musical institutions of symphony, opera, and ballet play in the whole fabric of our society — then we must fight for all of these. And the attempt to preserve these depends on you and me individually.

People will fight for and preserve what they determine to be valuable. Valuable music — and by that I mean music that enno-bles the human spirit or in some way enriches the human experi-ence — is not perceived as valuable by the vast majority of Amer-icans. To change this perception, the necessity of including music in the building of an educated and a complete human personality would have to be recognized. But the catch is that we have no right to argue that music is a necessity, especially in such economic times as these, unless the musical training and the musical material we are offering are truly valuable. That is why it is imperative to insist on quality — on thoroughly trained master teachers and on only the best-quality material. Over the past twelve years classroom and music teachers who recognize that children love the Kodály music class, but who are hostile to the idea of change, have repeatedly asked me why we can't use and apply all the "wonderful new Kodály techniques" — the hand signals and ti-ti tas — but with all the "good old songs" with which they are familiar. In other words, they want to have their cake and eat it, too. To accede to such requests is exactly what we must not do.

But there is something we *can* do, assuming we are careful to maintain an exacting standard in all our endeavors, and that is to broaden our base. To be recognized as valuable, Kodály-inspired music instruction on a high level must first become available to more segments of our society. In Hungary, Kodály's efforts ulti-mately were absorbed into the fabric of the society. Music there is in the day-care centers for six-month- to two-year-old babies; it forms a large part of nursery school and preschool curriculum; it continues by mandate (that is, it is not voluntary) beyond elemen-tary school into the junior and senior high schools; every little town has its culture house, where musical activities can be carried on, even until old age sets in. We cannot hope either to convert, or to make a high-quality Kodály experience available to, the broad mass of the American public — our country is simply too big. But we can investigate different types of population that would clearly benefit (learning disabled, prison and nursing home populations, etc.).

Let us consider some of the problems facing us in the 1980s:

the need for interglobal communication, understanding, and interaction; the extremes of wealth and poverty, which have led to apathy and hopeless despair; crime on a national scale, which is not confined to our large cities; the breakdown of the family; racial violence; the increase of children with learning disabilities and emotional disturbance; the loss of religious faith and decline of the churches; the decline of taste in all cultural matters, intensified by cheap commercialization and TV; the pathetic plight of the aged, not all of whom are indigent, whose children — even when affluent — more often than not consign them to the rubbish heap.

This is a pretty grim picture (and it does not even mention nuclear or environmental concerns), but try to turn it around for a moment to the opportunities such a picture presents for those of us who have been affected by Kodály's philosophy and are already adequately trained, or at least willing to acquire such training. Let us consider these problems in the context of the Kodály movement. Kodály has already made its impact on an international basis as a language of communication. I was aware of its potential in the field of international understanding when I took my original pilot class to Hungary in 1970 to make a film. These fourth- to eighth-grade children were unable to speak Hungarian but could communicate in the language of music, and I know that this international experience changed their lives. I know where they all are now, eleven years later, and I am proud of them as human beings.

As for the extremes of wealth and poverty, the Kodály approach has already demonstrated its value at both levels but is not yet totally accepted at either level. We must have more Sean Deiblers influencing the Ivy League circuit of preparatory schools such as Haverford, more acceptance of public school programs in systems as widely divergent as highly affluent West Hartford and racially violent, economically depleted Boston. These, along with a few well-established or developing programs, such as those in New Haven, San Jose, and Chattanooga, are good beginnings but only a pebble in the sea of need.

Consider the breakdown of the family or the difficulties experienced by two working parents. We haven't begun to explore the potential of Kodály in day-care centers, or the possibility of working with parents. Preschool private classes are beginning to mushroom in a few communities, but offer very little financial security to the teacher. Such classes need to get into the nurseries and kindergartens as basic core curriculum. Preschoolers and kindergartners are at an age when one can instill a permanent thirst for good music, when one can lay a foundation that will result in the kind of child who, emerging into adulthood, will feel incomplete without music in his or her life. Children exposed to Kodály instruction at this age cannot fail to be more sensitive, discerning individuals as they grow up. Japan has been very smart in its application of Kodály's principles — it elected to concentrate on kindergarten level and now has a wonderful base from which to expand.

We have not yet scratched the surface with learning-disabled, emotionally disturbed, or otherwise handicapped individuals. Lois Abeles's early research in the field of Kodály with learning-disabled children yielded provocative but inconclusive results that indicated the need for further investigation. The recent establishment of the international organization Music Education for the Handicapped (MEH), which invited me to speak on this subject in France in August 1980, together with IKS's invitation for me to speak on the same subject in Japan in August 1981, demonstrates that this field is one of not merely American but international concern. The problems are getting worse, not better, and we can no longer afford to turn them over to specialists. They are everyone's responsibility; following experimentation and the production of measurable results, facing these problems should be dealt with in our teacher training.

The problem of the decline of musical taste is a monstrous one, involving both TV and the stranglehold of the band movement on music education. Michael Murray, a discerning and enthusiastic promoter of the Kodály concept during his tenure at Boosey & Hawkes, has often said that if we want to effect changes in music education in this country, we must pay attention to the instrumental program, especially bands. I am not advocating the dissolution of bands; they are as American as apple pie and baseball, and to do so would be like attacking the concept of motherhood or democracy. I am saying, however, that we can and must try to influence the early steps in instrumental training; band directors need to be made aware of Kodály philosophy and techniques. The percentage of young adolescents who survive the American instrumental program beyond the state of out-of-tune and arrhythmic tootling to make it into the elite marching, concert, or symphonic bands is small — which means that a minority influences the direction of music education for the majority. It is all well and good for the few who make it to the glorious bespangled uniforms and the trip to the national conventions or the football games where thousands clap thunderous approbation of their colorful attire, clever arrangements, precise formations, and perfect performances. But what of the average little Johnny and Mary in the elementary school band whose starry eyes are shining with that distant dream, but whose lack of visible basic talent, combined with the often mindless type of instruction offered, will never allow them to reach that beloved, much sought-after goal? The instruments of their original choice and affection are nine times out of ten soon consigned to the attic, and they are turned off to real music for good, because their tastes have already been formed by the prestige of the bass-drum thumper and first trumpet — never mind how deafening or out of tune. We must not tolerate this situation any longer. Those of you who play band instruments, teach privately, or are in charge of band or orchestra programs need to apply what you learn from your Kodály training to your work, especially in the choice of materials.

We have not begun to investigate the potential of the Kodály concept in our churches, both at junior and senior choir level. We need to train choir conductors, children, and adults in Kodály choral techniques. The most beautiful literature in the world already exists for adult choirs; there is some good sacred music available for children's choirs, but more needs to be written that is both challenging and within the range of children's voices. The greatest difficulty here is in motivating already established conductors to learn about Kodály. Few of them know what a tremendous resource they have at their disposal in the Kodály movement. The best place to start is with the Kodály-trained music teacher who also holds a church choir position. If the quality of material and standard of performance are raised by such a teacher, both the minister and congregation will be quick to perceive it — perhaps not always to the benefit of the minister. In one church where our KCA Chamber Chorus sang year before last, a wayward parishioner was heard to say, "If that chorus would perform instead of the sermon every Sunday, I'd come to church regularly." That is not the result we are after; yet there is no denying that the church is another avenue to expand the Kodály potential.

The problems we face in the 1980s, both in music and in society at large, are greater than ever before, but so are the opportunities. These two, society and music, cannot be separated from each other. We can no longer afford the luxury of "art for art's sake" or to say, "We are musicians, we shouldn't involve ourselves in these other things (such as academic or societal issues). We should concern ourselves only with music." As far as teaching goes I agree. We should stick to the music, and it must not be watered down, fragmented, or degraded to fit a particular situation. Still, we must be more aware of the context in which we are teaching. We need to perceive that the music can be a tool or vehicle to achieve not only musical literacy but also a host of other important objectives necessary to living in today's world: aesthetic perception and taste, and an awareness of, concern for, and tolerance of one's fellow man — whatever his position in life.

We cannot all be involved in all of the problems and all of the opportunities; that would lead to the very fragmentation and dilution we seek to avoid. It is important to recognize that no one of us is a superman, that we need to encourage diversity but to insist on excellence in a field of our choice, and it is equally important to be joyous and thankful when someone else succeeds at something we have not dared to attempt or know we cannot do well. All of the various followers of Kodály philosophy have something valuable to offer for a particular constituency; the only criterion for admission to this friendly circle is the insistence on quality in our every effort. Not all of us will achieve this high quality in our results, and to demand that every result be of only the highest quality is not only a pipe dream but an elitist attitude we can ill afford. Nevertheless, we must never cease striving to reach for a high-quality result — it is the least we can ask of ourselves, for we value only those things for which we have had to struggle hard and which have been bought with sacrifice.

The problems are much more complicated now than in the past, and in the future they may become even greater. But our task is for the present. For today we must always be on the alert; we must listen carefully lest we miss any new thing that might help us, or fail to recognize any danger signals that might impede us. Above all, we must strive constantly to encourage, to accept, and to further, both in our own profession and in other fields of endeavor, the changes that record the progress of human history and the advances of civilization.

13. Kodály and the Quality of Life

This chapter is adapted from a speech delivered at a fund-raising dinner hosted by Dr. Louis Szathmáry, a KCA Associate Trustee, Chicago, May 8, 1981.

Zoltán Kodály is known in America mainly as a composer, mostly by conductors, orchestras, and choruses who too infrequently perform his works. His excellent concept of music education has only recently attracted national attention, and it may come as a surprise to learn that his concept is gaining recognition in areas other than music. Possibly even Sir Georg* may not know that educational psychologists, learning theorists, and those working in fields such as race relations and learning disabilities have become interested in it.

My own interest in the Kodály concept stemmed from my concern over the shrinking audience for serious music, the appalling lack of taste shown in the choice of materials to be used by music teachers in their classrooms, and the high degree of musical illiteracy everywhere — even among gifted students. Two discussions with Kodály, in the summers of 1965 and 1966, convinced me of the importance of studying his ideas at their source in Hungary. I went there in 1967–68, ostensibly to find a better way of music education, but found something far beyond that alone. I found an educational philosophy in which music education played a central role and yielded benefits other than music. I found that music was a synthesizing force in integrating the social, emotional, intellectual, and spiritual devel-

*Sir Georg Solti, a member of KCA's Sponsors Council, was in attendance at this fund-raising dinner.

tent, for Kodály believed in development. He believed that man and society could be reformed, and stood at all times for progress." [1] Kodály offers teachers the possibility of full development of native musical abilities, the fulfillment of individual potential, and immersion in something meaningful and worthwhile; for students it offers the possibility of success, observable progress in the development of basic skills (both musical and intellectual), and self-confidence.

In 1969, near the beginning of authentic Kodály activity in the United States, I wrote an article titled "Can the Kodály Method Be Successfully Adapted Here?" [2] Although I felt there was no real reason why it could not be adapted here, and did not agree with the criticism that it could succeed only in a controlled, state-directed society, I did suggest that the Kodály concept (which I called "method" then) represented values our society might not yet be ready to accept. That diagnosis turned out to be prophetically correct. As the Kodály concept became known and drew more and more followers, it was simultaneously attacked, as was Kodály himself a generation before in Hungary, for just those qualities for which its followers admired it most: order and sequence (heaven forbid — these inhibit creativity), literacy (we don't need it anymore — the printed word will become obsolete), use of only the most beautiful and valuable music (that is only for museums and not for the real world today), and a host of other objections. Our children were not to be taught; they were to absorb and flower naturally through pure creativity.

We have seen the result in the generation of "Why can't Johnny read?" children, whose teenage parents often can't manage their checkbooks either (purportedly that doesn't matter since we have calculators to solve our daily mathematical problems). The "flower children" generation was going to prevent future Vietnams; the world's soul was going to be made beautiful. We would discard the old repressive, restrictive customs and mores and create a new order. Yes, we have seen the result.

We have seen the breakdown of such institutions as marriage and the church; the breakdown of authority and a rejection of morals; decadence, the "eat, drink, and be merry for tomorrow we die" philosophy; lack of responsibility in government; loss of idealism and lack of public concern for one's fellow man; loss of faith in honesty and integrity. Everywhere is an appalling lack of taste and a sense of spiritual starvation. Money and power are our great gods. Where is the vision and leadership to cut through this confusion, focus our goals, and plan for the future?

One cannot find the answers in a movement or a cult; the seeds of change are to be found only deep within each individual. And here is where Kodály can help, for his entire life struggle in behalf of humanity was based first on promoting individual strength, dignity, freedom, and progress.

I believe we have had enough. The pendulum is swinging, and the criticisms leveled at the Kodály concept are beginning to recede — or perhaps I should say, its values are beginning to be recognized. For deeply imbedded in most human beings are feelings of decency and a longing for basic and eternal values. We are beginning to seek out these values and not be ashamed of them.

I will continue to warn against fanaticism on the part of disciples of the Kodály concept. Nothing will be accomplished by criticism of others' beliefs or excessive proselytizing of our own. At the same time I will continue to insist that Kodály's ideas, not his so-called "method," are timeless, like that of all great men and women, and have value for us as we struggle with a difficult and uncertain world today.

Which of his ideas, which elements of his philosophy can encourage, guide, and help us in these perilous times? Why can those trained in Kodály be hopeful?

First, we have the evidence of those who have received in-depth Kodály training, any one of whom will tell you it has changed their lives. They will tell you not only that their training gave them sharply increased musical skills and expanded resources on which to draw with children, but that in a broader, deeper sense, it gave them an ability to deal with life. Why? Because they were successful and knew they had something important to give the children and the adults they taught: in short, their lives are meaningful.

Kodály said, "Money does not produce ideas. . . . the most valuable things cannot be bought with money." [3] I can attest to those teachers having taken large financial risks to acquire Kodály training and to their having accepted scant financial remuneration to help establish KCA, and I believe they would tell you they are not sorry. They will tell you that the opportunity to help develop children's character and shape personality, to bring laughter, joy, a sense of identity, and self-respect to those whom they teach is worth more than money.

Kodály complained in Hungary that "public opinion ... believes that school and life are different things." [4] Today we know that these cannot be separated; they must be integrated. We know we must give children the tools to live in a real world — the ability to get along with others, the ability to discriminate and make choices, to reason logically, to develop permanent skills and habits of working. Good Kodály teaching does all of this for a child, and we have the opportunity to give children these gifts.

Kodály has taught us to strip away all sham, to stick only to what is true and reflects the real experience of living people. He has said that "powerful sources of spiritual enrichment spring from music." [5]

It is often in times of greatest stress — times such as these — that persons of ability and vision seem to emerge from the depths of blackness to lead others out of despair and inertia. The challenge is great, and the opportunity there. Will you be one of these? Most of those who have become leaders and master teachers in the American Kodály movement once thought of themselves as nothing but just another teacher — one in the crowd. But risk, commitment, and hard work have changed that for them — they have become invaluable disseminators of the American Kodály adaptation, performing a valuable service for American youth.

I would like to close with a story Jon Rappaport told me.* He recently bought fifty dollars' worth of records in a small record store. He wrote a check for the fifty dollars and asked the man be-

*A former director of the KCA summer courses and coordinator of academic programs.

hind the counter (who happened to be the owner of the store) if he wanted identification. The man replied no, that in the three and a half years since opening the store he had never had a check bounce. He figured that anyone who buys classical records is trustworthy.

This is not a story intended to extol the virtues of classical music above all other kinds of music. The man's customers had doubtless been buying jazz, pop, rock, and folk records too. The point is, no person whose soul is filled with music is going to rob, rape, destroy, or kill. We have a blueprint to lead others to beautiful music — music that ennobles the spirit and lifts the soul — if we will but follow it.

[1] László Eösze, *Zoltán Kodály: His Life in Pictures* (Budapest: Corvina Press, 1971), p. 21.

[2] Published in *MUSART*, April–May 1970.

[3] Zoltán Kodály, *Selected Writings* (Budapest: Corvina Press, 1974), p. 126.

[4] Ibid., p. 148.

[5] Ibid., p. 120.

15. The Human Value of the Kodály Approach

This chapter is adapted from the opening address for the Kodály Center of America's 1988 summer session.

I am frequently asked to explain Kodály in a nutshell — in one pithy sentence — as if one could reduce the lifetime goals, struggles, achievements, and impact of any great mind or revolutionary to an instant formula. Explain Galileo, Newton, Einstein, Christ, Confucius, Buddha? Whatever the field, those who have advanced the progress of civilization in either material or nonmaterial ways have been driven by forces larger than themselves and have poured forth streams of creativity whose sources remain a mystery.

In a 1982 speech delivered in Kecskemét as a part of the Kodály Centennial celebration I noted that Kodály had become practically a household word, in music education at least — a brand name, almost an inanimate object. How can one learn or teach "Kodály" as one drinks Coca-Cola or smokes Marlboros? I was outraged and insulted on his behalf, yet I was as guilty as everyone else in this respect. Only slowly did I realize that this notoriety was perhaps not as bad as it seemed on the surface. "Kodály" has been slowly absorbed into the mainstream, mainly because it has been controversial; people have either loved or hated it, and the status quo has feared it.

If one is exposed to a good model and invests enough time to learn what it really is, the immediate benefits become apparent in terms of personal musicianship, success in the classroom, musical understanding, and human values. Many saw the changes Kodály training wrought in both children and teachers but did not want to invest such time or money; some who were already successful in their own chosen approach felt their own way was being challenged and feared the competition the Kodály concept presented; still others saw a "quick fix" to their own musical and pedagogical problems and elected to get minimal training — a two-week visit to Hungary, a one-week summer workshop, or a two- or three-day convention exposure. These latter became overnight Kodály experts, giving lectures or in-service courses back in their hometowns. Others who observed the flash-in-the-pan results were sharply critical and perhaps rightly so.

One cannot acquire Kodály's brand of musicianship overnight or expect far-reaching results without sustained, systematic study and effort, because his way is sequential and all-encompassing. Kodály's goal was, as ours must be, to train — in his famous Schumann-inspired definition of good musicianship — the ears, mind, heart, and hands.

Although a generation has passed since the introduction of the Kodály concept to this country, and our society is vastly changed from what it was in the mid-1960s, the challenge and the promise of Kodály's way are still applicable to our times, perhaps even more so.

Everyone knows that education, by and large, at all levels and with too few exceptions, has pursued a consistently downhill path since World War II, and its decline has accelerated sharply since the mid-1960s. We have tried every possible solution, from schools without walls and open classrooms to "Sesame Street," and now computer-based education.

Music education is no exception in this parade. Unable to develop an American system of our own that can increase awareness, literacy, taste, and the enjoyment of music both as an art and in terms of human value, we have accepted the innovations of other countries that have sought solutions to their own problems. Thus the new life injected into our sterile, traditional American music education scene has come from Austria through the Orff concept,

Switzerland through the Dalcroze, Japan through the Suzuki, and Hungary through the Kodály — all of them concepts with something simultaneously unique and universal to offer us. All four have gained international acceptance.

In typically American fashion, we have elected to try to have the best of all worlds, and so the eclectic approach, combining all of these "methods" with our own traditional system (or, I should say, lack of system), has become the current rage. An eclectic approach — a smattering of this and that — will not solve the problem of creating a more informed, perceptive, and discriminating musical public to be the future audiences for serious music. I am not at all certain whether this problem can be helped or solved within the confines of music education as we know it.

Music education, as with all educational disciplines, is the victim of our society's current value system. The majority's perception of what is valuable in life, not only in this country but in many countries around the world, is in sharp conflict with the values that the Kodály concept represents.

In America we are uncomfortable about many things. There is a general malaise; we are nervous about the possibility of nuclear annihilation or bringing about our own extinction through our insistence on polluting the environment. We are overwhelmed with the problems of drugs, crime, violence, and AIDS, and we are even beginning to worry about being buried under billions of tons of waste produced by an overplasticized and packaged economy. The list of ills that society faces on a global basis is endless.

Along with "Where are we headed," one may well ask, "What is the sense of butting our heads against the stone wall of such monumental problems? What difference can you or I possibly make, on an individual basis?" I can't really answer that question — yet I know that it is only through personal, caring, responsible, individual effort that we can turn things around.

Why is the Kodály concept a bright, hopeful light in this sea of darkness?

People often ask what is unique about the Kodály concept. I

usually have answered, "Good materials, a logical sequence, and it works!" But I always leave unspoken that indefinable element which is its essence and which lies in its human values.

Zoltán Kodály himself was no great paragon of virtue — he was, in fact, a difficult, hard-hitting, and controversial person who immediately perceived and ruthlessly cut down the ego-centered arrogance and dilettantism of many of his colleagues and students. Those who came under this critical attack feared and hated him. He was even forced out of the Liszt Academy and lost his directorship at one point. But he stood firm in his demand for excellence and determination to achieve the things he wanted for his country.

Above all, Kodály cared about his people; he believed in their worth, their talents, and the capacity of his tiny nation to contribute to world culture. He understood instinctively that music was a universal language that could bring people together, although he was greatly surprised at Stanford University in 1966 (when I met him for the second time) that anyone might want to adapt his way of music education elsewhere.

The Hungarian people have a fascinating and tragic history of struggle against the domination of other cultures — Romans, Turks, the Austrian Hapsburgs, and more recently the Soviets. Hungary lost a good part of its territory through the apportionment of First World War spoils. Yet the Hungarian people's spirit has survived. The difficulties they have endured have simultaneously created strength and compassion in the basic Hungarian character.

This is not a eulogy on Hungarian character, which, as with people anywhere and everywhere, can often be evil as well as good, and is shaped by forces and circumstances beyond their control. But people tend to emulate great leadership; and so, because of Kodály, who was motivated by a pure and unselfish desire to accomplish better things for his countrymen, we in America have benefited from his legacy through those who have carried his torch. For me, the importance of this legacy lies in its human value — the knowledge that a tiny, troubled nation has been helped to live with dignity and courage through the gift of music in song and pride of heritage. This gives me hope for the future of our country —

Part Four

Controversies Surrounding the Kodály Concept

16. Kodály Illusions: Are They Delusions?

This chapter is adapted from a speech for Maryland Music Educators given on April 27, 1974.

There have been many developments in the Kodály concept since it was introduced to America by Mary Helen Richards in the early 1960s. Is it in a healthy state? Has it fulfilled its promise? Has it been adapted according to the spirit of Kodály's intentions? Can it hold its own in our society's present scale of values? What directions should it take in the future?

Every day more people are becoming interested in Kodály and convinced that it is the best way they know to educate musically. Certainly much has been accomplished already. Teachers have become aware that children can have a pleasurable musical experience in the classroom, that they can become musically literate. Folk music has been rediscovered as valuable material and found its way into many of the music series books on the market today. The Kodály International Symposium held in Oakland, California, in August 1973 brought together enthusiasts from all over the world. From this, from the increasing number of summer workshops and teacher-training programs, and from the many recent publications, one would conclude that the Kodály movement is certainly in a healthy state, going full steam ahead. But *how* is it going ahead? In the opinion of some teachers and musicians who were close to Kodály himself and who are dedicating their lives to carrying out his ideas, the movement is still far from fulfilling its promise. Why is this so? For three reasons, I believe.

1. People do not really know Kodály's ideas; they have substituted some of the techniques and tools of the so-called method (such as hand signals and ti-ti *tas*) for the basic philosophy. This is not their fault, for they have not been sufficiently exposed to the authentic concept to know what the basic philosophy is.
2. It is a common American trait, when something is good, to want to acquire it immediately, even though everyone knows that almost nothing of significant or permanent value is acquired without struggle, sacrifice, and hard work.
3. It is not at all certain that the real Kodály concept can exist in our present society's scale of values: if we want what it represents, we will have to fight for it.

The time has come to strike hard against those misconceptions concerning the Kodály concept that threaten to retard or destroy its promise. All kinds of people — university professors, heads of music education departments, influential composers, and school administrators — make flat statements that are taken for fact by an all too gullible and passive music educators' profession. The concept is both praised to the skies and severely attacked. It seems almost impossible to get an accurate picture of the true state of affairs regarding Kodály. Partially, this is because there are inadequate lines of communication, but in some cases, it is because what is taught under the Kodály banner is such a travesty that no consistent musical result can be seen, and even worse, that the philosophy behind the concept cannot be recognized.

Some of the misconceptions that follow are completely false, while others contain half-truths that only serve to confuse. We must fight the false impressions by example and listen carefully to the half-truths; they sound a warning to us to weed out or improve what is poor and to search for better solutions. In other words, we must be self-critical.

who are competent in both approaches may wish to use techniques of the two in combination, but the mere use of Orff instruments or body movements does not constitute Orff any more than hand signals and *ta ti-ti ta* constitute Kodály. Each approach can help the other when certain facets are employed in a supplementary sense, but let us do away with the nonsense that the mishmash creation of an "Orff-Kodály method" can give us our cake and allow us to eat it too. Such a dilution can only result in a weakening of the basic concepts of these two very fine composers. This is not a tirade against the Orff movement; in fact, Kodály people have a great deal to learn from Orff, which could expand the already evident strengths of Kodály and help in combating some of the accusations leveled at it. I ask that we stop deluding ourselves that we can teach successfully with the gimmicks of *any* method. We must realize that our most important task is to become the best musicians possible.

■ Relative Do Can't Be Used By Instrumentalists

Again, false. Relative *do* is *very* useful to instrumentalists. Most teachers who believe only in fixed *do* received their training in conservatories or universities from European music professors. That training, using fixed-*do* solfege, produced a fantastic ability to sight-read among gifted students. In this country the old-fashioned way of using movable *do*, fashionable thirty to fifty years ago, was for the most part boring, ineffectual, and intensely disliked. There were a few places, notably in the Midwest and in the Boston area, where an effective type of movable-*do* solfege (very close to current Kodály solfege) was taught. But its advocates were neither strong, numerous, nor vocal enough to start a movement that could permanently establish this successful system of sight-reading and ear training. Current animosity springs from

1. The disdain of teachers who are successfully using the fixed-*do* system.
2. The threat to those who are using fixed *do* unsuccessfully.
3. The miserable memories of those whom the old movable-*do* system has prejudiced against anything that might bear similarities.

[145]

- *A Month-Long Summer Workshop or a Two-Month Visit to Hungary Is Training Enough to Qualify a Person as a Kodály Expert*

This is false. A person should not claim he is qualified to teach in a Kodály manner unless he is a good musician, unless he has either been to Hungary or studied with current Hungarian or American master teachers for an appreciable length of time (a year, for instance), unless he has used the method himself in the classroom, and unless he is prepared to deal with the problem of material.

- *Kodály Will Teach Children How to Read the English Language*

This, of course, is quite absurd. The Kodály Musical Training Institute's cautious first steps into transfer effects caused an explosion of interest and resulted in the very thing we wish to guard against — extravagant claims. Kodály does train the ears to a high degree, with the result that children's inner hearing is developed and their ability to deal with phonics is improved. Therefore, children who are trained in Kodály have an advantage and *may* read better; in fact, the Institute's early experimental research seems to indicate that Kodály-trained children do read better. But perhaps an equally or even more important reason for such children reading better is the motivation they have acquired toward learning in general, the concentration they have developed, and the attitudinal and behavioral changes that may have taken place as the result of a pleasurable learning experience in Kodály.

- *Kodály Is Old-Fashioned and Doesn't Recognize the Value of, or Make Use of, Contemporary Music*

This is only partially true, but it is also at present one of the Kodály movement's weaker aspects. The Kodály concept is not old-fashioned. Kodály's ideas can be used at any time, in any place. Kodály would have been the first to go further, had he lived, and his widow is attempting now to convince all those with whom she comes in contact, especially Hungarian teachers, that they must not be complacently satisfied with the results achieved to date. But there are two important considerations to be faced before we can deal with the problem of contemporary music:

1. The average music educator has little knowledge, background, or training in twentieth-century music.
2. Since one of Kodály's strongest beliefs was that a child must be given only the best, it is necessary to distinguish the valuable and lasting from that which is merely in vogue. The problem is that a time lag of fifteen or twenty years is almost always necessary to make that distinction. Who could have been sure, even twenty years ago, that Charles Ives's music would someday find its way into American Series songbooks?

The challenge of contemporary music is that, as our knowledge accumulates and expands, what we give our children from both past and present becomes more and more a matter of wise choosing — there is too much literature, almost too many exciting avenues of approach, and not enough time. Imagine the difference between a child learning U.S. history in 1930 and in 1976. It is staggering! If one adds the rest of the world's history, the problem becomes even more acute. The same is true of every field, because of expanded media and communication. Can (or should) we throw our children into the present confusion of world musics, eclectic approaches, and current trends, into a sea of vast and overwhelming noises, with the hope they will emerge at the end of their high school or college experience with an ability to choose for themselves that which will most enrich their lives? Can we assume that the individual involvement, the creativity that we are attempting to foster, will be carried over into adult life, or will it be left behind in the classroom? Will our children be able to discriminate? Who knows? The Manhattanville, electronic, and aleatory people are every bit as dedicated as are Kodály enthusiasts, and looking just as hard for answers — which brings me to the last and greatest misconception about Kodály.

[147]

- ## The Most Important Aspect of the Kodály Concept Is Its Sequential Methodology; or, The Giant Misconception: Kodály = Methodology = Music

Methodology is exactly what the Kodály concept is not. Such a notion is the worst of all the misconceptions because it is the one that has already done and is likely to do the most damage in the future. Though it is true that the type of sequential methodology used in Kodály teaching can result in a high degree of musical skill for average children, the building of musical skills is not the ultimate goal of such a program. Unfortunately, many Kodály teachers think it is. To find a good methodological sequence must seem like a dream come true to the teacher who inadvertently stumbles onto the Kodály method. Naturally she (or he) wants it right away and thinks Kodály is the answer to all her problems. She attends workshops, buys books, and blindly follows a sequence with which some other Kodály teacher appears to have had success. If the first results are gratifying, she is likely to redouble her zealous efforts, not realizing that the progress produced by a master teacher through constantly varied repetition turns out to be dull drill in her hands and may not be as gratifying to the children as it is to her, their teacher. Those who oppose the Kodály concept criticize its sequential methodology more than any other aspect of the concept: this sequence is at once one of its greatest strengths and its greatest danger. Used as an end in itself, the methodology is a subversion of the whole Kodály philosophy. The critics are partially right, to the extent that a great many disciples of Kodály's ideas substitute the methodology for music. Now we are really down to brass tacks, for there is the essence of the Kodály idea — Music, with a capital M.

CONCLUSIONS

Those who want to teach according to Kodály's philosophy must face many problems as a result of the misconceptions here discussed. One of the most serious problems is that there are not enough good examples to follow, because the whole Kodály idea took off at too

little sympathy for city problems; budget cuts that threaten to destroy the morale of teachers and the quality of educational programs; and on top of it, administrators who, faced with declining scores in basic subjects necessary for survival in a society that is economically oriented, cut out the arts as nonessential frills. No one wants to assume responsibility for this state of affairs, preferring to leave it to the traditional educational and legislative authorities.

Looking down the road to the future, what kind of a world will our children face, or we ourselves in our so-called golden years, if the products of today's society are in control of education, business, and politics?

Although it is almost too discouraging to fight these problems alone, together we can do a lot more than we think we can. We must act now; we must individually and collectively concern ourselves with possible solutions to these problems. As far as the Kodály idea is concerned, we can no longer be content with trying to bring to the United States what I saw in Hungary in 1967. Nothing ever stays the same, and the beautiful results achieved through Kodály's efforts in Hungary are already being eroded there by a growing concern with meeting Western economic standards. Nevertheless, we have a priceless example in the Hungarian model, which is based on thorough, quality training. Whether the Kodály concept will survive as a fine way of teaching music in America is much less important than whether it can be successfully used by enough teachers and children to make an inroad on the many problems we face with those we teach.

The realities ahead of us this year are both frightening and challenging. The obstacles that threatened our survival and that frequently seemed incapable of solution in the past five months have one by one been overcome. Though we have not enough in material goods (either furniture or money!), we have nearly everything else going for us to make a success if our determination is great enough, and if we work hard enough. I cannot begin to tell you of the sacrifices that have been made by people in this room to preserve the standards and the spirit of KMTI. I am profoundly grateful to every person here today for commitment and sacrifice, both past and present, and I am particularly grateful to our three teaching fellows,† who were willing to risk personal security and established teaching careers without being certain of exactly what lay ahead. Their action is inspiring and encouraging to the rest of us, because it says we are starting KCA with quality. One of our country's great educators, John Gardner, has said that those of us who are most deeply devoted to a democratic society must be precisely the ones who insist upon the highest standards of performance and that the idea for which this nation stands will not survive if the highest goal that free men can set themselves is an amiable mediocrity. We must constantly fight this easy, comfortable way out, for it will surely destroy us in the end. Though excellence involves self-discipline and tenacity of purpose, we need not fear it, for where excellence exists is also to be found the release of human potential, the enhancement of individual dignity, and the liberation of the human spirit. To what greater goals can we ask to commit our lives and energies?

This year will not be easy for any of us, but we must give our best, and many hopes will rise and fall on the success of our efforts.

The opportunity is here and is great. I would finish this speech with a beautiful quote from Dag Hammarskjöld's book *Markings*, which I hope will help guide you as a beacon light over the inevitable rough spots during the coming year: "Never let success hide its emptiness from you, achievement its nothingness, toil its desolation. And so keep alive the incentive to push on further, that pain in the soul which drives us beyond ourselves." [3]

[1] Og Mandino, *The Greatest Salesman in the World* (New York: Fell, 1965), pp. 84, 89, 34.

[2] Zoltán Kodály, *Selected Writings* (Budapest: Corvina Press, 1974), p. 126.

[3] Dag Hammarskjöld, *Markings* (New York: Knopf, 1969), p. 55.

†Sheila Ryan, Barry Finnell, and Jim Fritz.

19. Kodály for Large Cities: The Boston Experience

This chapter is adapted from a paper read at the Music Educators National Conference's Eastern Division Convention, February 24, 1983. The paper was subsequently published in Massachusetts Music Educators News 32, no. 3 (1984).

The Boston experience with the Kodály approach to music education spans a period of thirteen years since 1970, in seventeen schools covering six of Boston's nine districts. We have worked with four-year-olds through ninth-grade level and hope to attempt an elective program at senior high level in the near future.

We now know, from the teachers we have trained who report to us regularly from a variety of teaching situations nationwide, that Kodály music approaches are successful in suburban and rural areas. We know that Kodály works for all ages, from two-year-olds and their parents to adult beginners, and to college instructors who teach musicianship and ear-training classes; that it helps advanced singers and instrumentalists heading toward a professional concert career; and that it is helpful with learning-disabled children and can be used with the physically handicapped.*

Why has the Kodály Center of America chosen to place a major emphasis on programs for inner-city children? The most important answer is that the special problems of urban life are so great that

*This last point is discussed in "Kodály Music for Learning-Disabled Children" (paper read at the Fifth International Kodály Symposium, Sapporo, Japan, August 1981) and in "Using the Kodály Approach with Emotionally Disturbed Children" (paper read at the Fourth International Music Education for the Handicapped Symposium, Goldwater Memorial Hospital, New York, N.Y., August 1985).

if we do not lay the seeds now, today's city children many never know the joy of music in their lives or experience its benefits.

What *are* the benefits to children of a good Kodály program anywhere? They can be enormous — first of all musically, but also intellectually, socially, emotionally, and spiritually. The acquisition of music literacy requires the development of basic skills that are useful for learning anything — attentiveness, concentration, and the ability to analyze, discriminate, and memorize. The reading and the writing of music are abstractions one step higher than the reading and writing of one's native language. The development of inner hearing and listening skills is fundamental to the reading process; rhythmic training is invaluable preparation for math.

Kodály techniques generally correspond to developmental learning theories; they employ, both separately and collectively, aural, visual, and motoric modes of learning. Children learn accuracy, permanently internalize basic concepts, and thus acquire confidence through constant repetition and going from known to unknown. They acquire patience (learning their turn will come), tolerance, and good social behavior in the circle games, which also give them a strong sense of identity (in the sense of "being chosen" to be in the center or to run around the outside of the circle).

They acquire a strong sense of responsibility through realizing that their individual participation has an important effect for good or bad on the performance produced by the rest of the group. Thus they come to understand the concept of excellence and that they are capable of it; they learn to respect the contribution of their peers and gain a sense of their own self-respect. The problem of discipline is diminished by success, and a healthy self-discipline is substituted. A good Kodály program will provide a safe emotional outlet and result in a child's eager anticipation and pure enjoyment of the music class.

If these are the benefits of a good Kodály program, what are the special urban problems in Boston? Many of the following problems are present in other large American cities, so perhaps KCA's experience may be helpful to music educators in other cities.

Opera Institute students on this campus† and those in the KCA course. In our first year here, KCA gave a demonstration of the type of skills acquired in Kodály training, from beginning to advanced levels, and ended with a humorous but very difficult choral take-off, complete with soloists, on operatic style. The Goldovsky opera people were thunderstruck — their estimate of the Kodály music program skyrocketed, and respect for Kodály-trained teachers increased 100 percent overnight. Many of them inquired how they could get such training for themselves. But this was quickly forgotten.

KCA students of former summer courses have sometimes complained that they have been considered second-class citizens here by Opera Institute students and personnel; if so, I believe we have only ourselves to blame. Railing against the unjust jibes of prima donnas will not solve the situation. We *can* point to the fact that the greatest artists have frequently been the greatest teachers and have also been committed to excellence in public education — performers like Sir Yehudi Menuhin, Isaac Stern, Rudolf Serkin, and Luciano Pavarotti; did you know that the latter was once an elementary school music teacher himself? These great men have not considered music education beneath their dignity, because they have understood the need for and the power of good music and good education to develop the mind, shape the personality and character, and educate the heart. That is why artists such as those who have given their names to KCA's Sponsors Council support the Kodály philosophy. Doráti, Ormandy, Solti, Menuhin, Serkin, Vásáry, Ferencsik — all knew Kodály personally and knew that he both represented and demanded excellence and that he was a visionary who saw in music the possibility of effecting changes and values in society at a grass-roots level.

We can be grateful that Kodály achieved what he did in Hun-

---

†Southeastern Massachusetts University. KMTI's summer course was held at Wellesley College 1973–76. KCA's summer course was held at Southeastern Massachusetts University 1978–85; at the Kodály Institute in Kecskemét, Hungary, 1986 and 1989, and as part of the Great Woods Educational Forum and Music Festival in Norton, Massachusetts, 1987 and 1988.

gary and that he left a legacy from which many other nations have already benefited. We must always honor and respect him for his contribution to music education and humanity at large; at the same time we must move forward in both thought and action to solve the problems of our time. This does not mean discarding the past — it means understanding and sifting through it, retaining the best of it, and expanding the basic ideas creatively to fit current conditions and needs.

We are living on the edge of a volcano that could erupt and obliterate us all at any moment. The entire world is searching for a way out of the mess we have gotten ourselves into. We are in desperate need of balance, law, order, and respect for human life and dignity. To bring it down to the small orbit of our musical world, we do not need the destructive force of competitive ideologies each struggling to achieve dominance over the others; we need to shed the dog-eat-dog mentality of the small child who says to his next-door neighbor, "My father is better than yours because he has a bigger car and makes more money than yours," or the parent who says, "My daughter can't play with Mrs. Astor's daughter because the Astor family has Rolls-Royces and yachts, and my daughter can't entertain Mrs. Astor's daughter in the same way."

Music educators must stop feeling inferior and sorry for themselves and must develop their individual abilities to their fullest potential in order to know they have something of value to give; performers must stop giving the impression that music educators are the lowest rung of the musical ladder and must realize that their God-given gifts will amount to nothing if there is no one there to receive them and to listen; they need also to develop their ears, minds, and hearts as well as their fingers and lungs in order to have something to give other than mere velocity or high Cs.

For fifteen years I have been trying to draw public attention to the value of Kodály's ideas and to encourage both teachers and students to become trained. I may have done so too forcefully, however, because one of the besetting sins of many who receive Kodály training is that, in their enthusiasm, they attempt to convince others of the value of the Kodály concept. If you like what you received here, go out and use it, be the best teacher you possibly can, but don't say you are teaching Kodály, for you are not — you are teaching music! And furthermore, you are not just teaching music — you are teaching *people* music.

Plato said, "The man who has music in his soul will be most in love with the loveliest." Today's world needs so much to be in love with the loveliest. Here, for a few weeks, we have a chance to live by and with that truth. May the days ahead fulfill both your musical expectations and your inner personal needs.

21. The Adaptation of Kodály's Ideas to Another Culture

This chapter is adapted from a paper written for the Seventh International Kodály Symposium, London, England, July 1985.

When I first heard Zoltán Kodály and Professor Erzsébet Szönyi speak at Stanford University in California in 1966, I was both inspired and overwhelmed with the implications of Kodály's ideas for U.S. society. The result of my encounters with those charismatic personalities was that I spent a year of intensive study in Hungary in 1967–68. When I returned to the United States the following August, I had stars in my eyes: I was going to make sweeping changes in American music education overnight; I was going to cause a musical revolution; I was going to create a generation of musically literate children. How naïve I was! I had no idea of the obstacles and pitfalls that lay ahead or the discouragements I would encounter. In fact, it is only now, some seventeen years later, that I am finally understanding the main reason adapting Kodály's ideas in America has been so frustrating: namely, that they are basically contrary to our culture.

As stated earlier, Kodály said that the greatest trouble is not the emptiness of the purse but the emptiness of the soul. America says the greatest trouble is the emptiness of the wallet and doesn't worry too much about the emptiness of the soul. Kodály said no man is complete without music — America says no man is complete without two cars in his garage and a $50,000 bank account. Kodály said that only the best is good enough for children and that only art of intrinsic value is suitable for children, yet consider what worthless pap is presented in colorful extravaganzas via the television tube in an effort to educate the minds and hearts of children to the need for and desirability of products offered by Madison Avenue. Kodály said that powerful sources of spiritual enrichment spring from music. Our country has plenty of evidence that the wrong kind of music is a powerful source of violence and crime.

One could continue with a long list of entrenched values in American society (and probably most Western ones) that have made it difficult to adapt Kodály's ideas in our country. It was because I was concerned with the emptiness of our value system that I wanted to introduce Kodály's ideas into our culture and to educate a generation of children whose hearts and minds would be programmed to feel, think, and act differently.

In September 1968, although I had become aware of vast cultural differences between our two countries from my year in Hungary, these were not my main concern; I was inspired, excited, enthusiastic, and impatient to start my new work. I went at it with almost fanatic zeal. As with every new venture, especially one backed by such an influential and prestigious body as the Ford Foundation, tremendous interest and publicity was generated overnight. Everyone wanted a piece of the pie, everyone wanted to know how to go to Hungary, and quite naturally, everyone assumed our young new Institute was rolling in Ford Foundation money and would provide them scholarships to go. However, anyone who has ever dealt with the Ford Foundation knows that is not the way it works — every penny must be accounted for long before one even receives notification of the grant.

As awareness of the Kodály concept grew in our country, doubts and skepticism also emerged. Music teachers brought up in the traditional approach began to attack this new revolutionary way of music education. Many misconceptions grew up as a result of the faulty information and half-truths garnered from the overnight Kodály experts with little or no training.

Along about 1973, five years after returning from my year's study in Hungary, I realized that the honeymoon was over. The period of interest in a new idea had passed and it was time to face the music. We would have to face the problems these misconceptions represented, especially because there was an element of truth to some of them. In a speech delivered to the Maryland Music Educators eleven years ago, in April 1974 (see chapter 16), I said that it was not at all certain that the real Kodály concept could exist in our society's scale of values — that if we wanted what it represents, we would have to fight for it.

Those who want to adapt Zoltán Kodály's ideas for music education in Western countries will have to fight for them and be prepared to struggle; to work often in unfriendly atmospheres; to accept the taunts and criticisms of colleagues who are threatened by the successes of teachers trained in and committed to Kodály's philosophy of music education; and to ignore the petty jealousies of teachers with varying degrees of training within the Kodály movement itself, who disagree as to how Kodály's "method" should be adapted. We have to answer the questions of skeptical school superintendents and other school authorities who have been led to believe that Kodály music training will improve reading scores but do not see this result. Funding sources grill us on why Kodály's way of music education is better than any other music method, on why it deserves a place in the core curriculum or should be considered important in the total development of an individual human personality.

The problem of funding is a crucial one for Western countries wanting to adapt Kodály's way of music education to their own cultures. Because our government allots so little to education, let alone the arts, we are dependent, when introducing new educational curricula or philosophies, on foundations, a few corporations, and wealthy individuals for funding support, and the competition for dollars from these sources is fierce. Who is going to give money for even a good type of music education when people are dying of starvation the world over and when the need to eliminate the possibility of nuclear destruction is so overwhelming? Why should the brightest and best of our youth graduating from colleges, universities, and music schools elect a career in music education — even

able, even after seventeen years, to produce a sequential public school model (public in the American sense) that even begins to approximate what is possible or what should be expected. As explained earlier, the basic problems of our culture are seemingly huge obstacles in the path, but the prize is worth struggling for and winning.

It seems to me that a basic question for the IKS as it continues to spread interest and gain new friends all over the world is this: Is the Kodály method, approach, system, philosophy — call it what you will — only an excellent way of *music* education? Or does it have larger goals? Did Kodály give up composing masterpieces mainly to create the best music education possible, or was his principal goal to bring human beings to a greater sense of individual self-worth and into better communication with each other? As the King of Siam says in *The King and I*, "Is a puzzlement." We do know that Kodály said that music making is not an end in itself, but must stand at the service of the whole people. Whatever the answer, Kodály has blazed a trail by showing us a way to ennoble the human spirit through feeding and nurturing it with beautiful music. The rest is up to us.

1 KCA Chamber Chorus in a Museum of Fine Arts concert, Boston, 1978. The group includes the four members of KCA's first class: Sheila Ryan, Jim Fritz, Just Holm, and Barry Finnell. Back row: F. Lund, unidentified, J. Sanders, V. Loebell, S. Holm, S. Ryan, L. Kidson, D. Bacon. Front: J. Fritz, unidentified, J. Rappaport, K. Knighton, B. Finnell.

2 Faculty and administration of the first KCA summer course, Southeastern Massachusetts University, 1978: J. Fülöp, L. Bodolay, E. Sipos, J. Rappaport, V. Loebell, L. Gábor, D. Bacon, J. Sanders, E. Vendrei, I. Kainen, S. Deibler, D. Block, B. Miller, F. Lund.

3 Members of the first Kodály "College Level Theory Course" taught by Erzsébet Hegyi, summer 1979. J. Boutin, C. Bethel, P. Ambush, L. Bodolay, P. Tacka, M. O'Neill, B. Bertaux.

4 KCA headquarters 1983–1990, 295 Adams Street, Newton, Massachusetts.

5 KCA board chairpersons, 1977–1993. Right to left: John Patterson (1977–1987), Charles Drake (1988–1989), Judith Fülöp and Joel Slocum (co-chairpersons 1989–1992, Slocum chairperson 1992–). Not shown: Cynthia Healer, acting chairperson 1987–88.

6 Denise Bacon with her revered teacher, Mieczyslaw Horszowski, 1966.

7 Denise Bacon performs Grieg's Piano Concerto with the Boston Pops Orchestra, 1962.

8 Sarolta Kodály and Istvan Lantos, Kodály Centennial benefit concert for KCA, Longy School of Music, 1982.

9 Csaba Onczay, artist in residence at KCA summer course, 1980–1984.

10 Denise Bacon and Mrs. Kodály in performance, 1980 summer course, Southeastern Massachusetts University.

11 Sarolta Kodály and violinist Dénes Zsigmondy following 1967 Budapest concert. Zsigmondy also gave a benefit for the pilot class trip to Hungary.

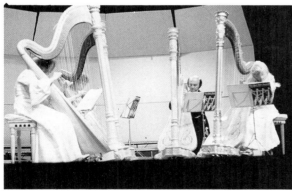

12 Michalis Patseas introduces Denise Bacon, who gave a seminar on "Why Kodály Training for Pianists," 11th International Kodály Symposium, Athens, Greece, 1989.

13 New York Harp Ensemble benefit concert at 1983 summer course, Southeastern Massachusetts University.

Part Five

The Kodály-Trained Teacher: "Trained Ears, Mind, Heart, and Hands"

22. The Authentic Kodály Concept and Teacher Training

This chapter is adapted from a paper read at the New York State Music Conference, 1973.

The question of authenticity versus too quick or too superficial adaptations is one that has plagued almost every big movement through the ages. Look at Montessori or the new math, for instance. One can agree or disagree with a concept, but only if one knows what it is. The problem with the Kodály concept is that music educators all over the country heard about it, became excited about it, and immediately used bits and pieces of it, thereby creating a reputation for it long before any example of the real thing was established. Yet many people still do not know what it really is.

Several people have been to Hungary for two or three days, two or three weeks, or even two or three months. They come home inspired and want the same result they have seen in Hungary. They are surprised when they can't get it and their followers become disillusioned, concluding that the concept is all well and good in a state-directed society, but that it won't work here. Or they have moderate success, if they are good enough musicians, but those who copy them often do not succeed.

There are at least four reasons that explain the instances of failure with the Kodály concept in this country. First, the teacher trying to use it may himself not be a good enough musician. Second, he may be a good musician but have not enough training in the concept. Third, he may both be a good musician and have adequate training, but be unable to communicate with children. Fourth, he may be in too unsympathetic a situation to achieve results — his school system may not be ready for it. Moreover, at present our society itself may not want the values the Kodály concept represents.

What are some of these values? The ability to think, to reason, to evaluate, to discriminate, to have an independent opinion, to be unafraid of feeling, to seek and appreciate the beautiful, to reject what is trash or in poor taste, to strive for excellence and perfection, to recognize the special abilities and disabilities of others and to be tolerant of them. Such attributes are not very popular with the youth cult right now or even with the parent generation.

What are the hallmarks of authentic Kodály teaching?

1. A teacher who is a good musician, whose inner hearing is highly developed, but who constantly seeks to improve his own musicianship

2. An adequately trained teacher who has studied with current Hungarian or American master teachers, either in Hungary or in this country, and who knows how to develop a pedagogical sequence of musical elements to be taught from the lowest level regardless of the level at which he is currently teaching

3. A teacher who knows a large body of authentic American folk songs; who, through analysis, can identify a good folk song when he sees or hears one; who knows and is willing to use the folk songs of varied ethnic groups and many countries at the appropriate age level; and who knows appropriate art music for various levels of teaching

4. A teacher who loves music and has a need to participate in live music making

5. Enjoyment by the children of the music itself and of the conscious learning of musical elements in the lesson (this can be seen in the expressions on their faces)

6. Children who can sing in tune, who are rhythmically accurate, who can read and write music at a level appropriate to their age and frequency of instruction, and who can use musical symbols for their own improvisation

7. A teacher who is willing to make sacrifices, who is willing to put in the time necessary to prepare lessons adequately, and who seems to be committed to something beyond music education or personal career objectives

If some of these attributes of authentic Kodály teaching seem idealistic, let me say they are, but they are not unobtainable. Many people trained in KMTI's one-month summer courses say they never realized they had so much latent ability or that they could feel so committed to an idea.

Having previously detailed the reasons why Kodály is not always successful, let me mention the reasons why it usually is successful.

First, because it is directly challenging to an individual's basic potential and requires him to expand it continuously. Kodály's goal was to bring each person to his own highest potential, not to make professional musicians of everyone by an absolute standard. Too often, a teacher's own musical worth lies dormant — unused, untapped. His university or conservatory training is all but forgotten (unless perchance he becomes a conductor at a fairly advanced level). School authorities usually expect or require nothing other than that the music teacher keep order in the classroom and give the classroom teacher a break in her daily schedule. Kodály training gives a teacher a glimpse of his own potential as well as the desire to live up to it.

Second, the Kodály teacher has a good chance to succeed because he is far more than the usual one or two steps ahead of the child. Kodály said that one has to work hard to be good enough to teach little children. Whether one teaches small children or university students, the Kodály teacher is expected to be capable of teaching at either extreme. Those who studied with Péter Erdei two years ago at our Institute, or visitors who watched him teach second-grade children, were astonished when he returned from Hungary this past summer to our course at Wellesley College and brilliantly conducted an entire program, from memory, with Boston's Cantata Singers. Yet this young man was the product of the music education division of the Liszt Academy when he first started to teach, here in this country, in 1968.

[193]

Third, Kodály can succeed because the success element is built into the teaching process. Preparation is the key, and children are led to discover consciously that for which they have been prepared unconsciously, only after they have experienced it and need to find a name for it.

Fourth, Kodály can succeed because it is based on the genuine expression of real people — namely, folk music, which is the distillation of various times and regions — rather than on utilitarian music composed all too often by a not too talented teacher or professor to fit a pedagogical purpose. Furthermore, the folk music is a bridge and logical step to art music, which once experienced and understood, is the permanent possession and treasure of the child.

This point of view will be attacked by those who say serious music, or music that can be defined as classic because it has withstood the test of time, belongs in museums and is not for today's children. On the same basis one might say that only Watergate itself is important now, that one need not know anything of past history to interpret or deal with it. Perhaps succeeding generations or centuries will record the folk music of a Watergate period. To what will that music have led? Paul Henry Lang, one of the greatest music historians of our country, felt that with the decline of the Roman Empire, music deteriorated to the point of being little more than mere gratification of the senses. Let us fight a similar situation in our time with every measure at our disposal.

In conclusion: about two hundred to three hundred teachers have now been exposed to KMTI training. Several more are being exposed to authentic training at various two- and three-week summer courses where the Institute is able to send a qualified Hungarian master teacher. The teachers who receive this training will be able to effect significant changes in their school systems. But what is urgently and desperately needed is more American *master* teachers to replace the Hungarian master teachers, to train those who are teaching in schools. I see the future training of Kodály teachers as taking place in two different directions and, I hope, in the same institution — perhaps a four-year undergraduate institution of the quality of a Curtis Institute, but for music educators. Those two directions should be (1) to develop a few master teachers of the highest quality, who in turn will be able (2) to train that great body of committed music specialists who will teach the children of the next generation to be more sensitive individuals. Impossible? I don't believe so.

23. Quality Teacher Training Through the Kodály Approach

This chapter is adapted from a paper read at the Third International Kodály Society Symposium, Halifax, Nova Scotia, August 1977, and subsequently published in the IKS Bulletin, 1977, nos. 1–2.

Clearly, when talking of Kodály and teacher training in the same breath, what we are all after is the result we have seen and heard, or heard about, in Hungary. How can we obtain such a result for our own countries? Obviously, we must train teachers who, we hope, will one day be able to produce the same result.

Many musical institutions in America are producing respectable musicians and good teachers, but the magic we have seen in Hungary is, for the most part, not being transmitted to our children.

Of what is that magic born? It is a difficult thing to put one's finger on and could be attributed to a host of sociological, economic, and political factors. In the end it is the direct communication and interaction of teacher and student, parent and child, on which real education must depend. Kodály said that "as a general rule, only someone who has been taught well can teach well" [1]; also, he stated in 1949, "increased production of quality is what the aim must be. . . . this is in the interests of the community, of culture, of our country and the duty of everyone." [2]

It is my task today to suggest what constitutes quality training through the Kodály approach. To start with, I must decry the notion that our objective is to produce a "Kodály teacher" — in my opinion, there is no such thing. Our objective should be to produce a well-equipped teacher who can in-

24. Kodály Training: Musicality or Gymnastics?

This chapter is adapted from a paper read at the Organization of American Kodály Educators Conference, Bloomington, Indiana, March 1980.

The members of the KCA faculty represent a large geographic spread and have taught in both public and private education at all grade levels from preschool through college and conservatory. Whatever their background and irrespective of their teaching situation, they consistently voice the same complaint — namely, that we are so concerned with superficial gimmicks leading to quick success in the classroom that we may be missing the whole point of our involvement in the Kodály concept.

Our faculty came to the conclusion last summer that we may be guilty of producing teachers who are more concerned with mechanical gymnastics in "musical literacy" than with musicality in performance and cultivating an understanding and love of music itself. The main point of this paper is to suggest that musical gymnastics, important as they are in developing musical literacy, must be at the service of the music itself, rather than engaged in for their own sake.

Too often Kodály-trained teachers have been stuffing their students' brains but not feeding their souls. In the process, we as teachers may produce brilliant results in the eyes of visitors to our classrooms, but of what use is it for children to be able to sing a folk song interchangeably in sol-fa, numbers, and letter names, tell its form, perform it from memory with a complicated ostinato, write it down,

[201]

transpose it to other keys, identify it from hearing its rhythm clapped or hearing its melody internally, by reading it silently from book or chalkboard — what good is it, if they cannot also forget all of this and enjoy the song because of its sheer beauty, exuberance, humor, or whatever is most characteristic of it? What good are all the gimmicks that lead to musical literacy, if in the end, children know everything about a song, technically speaking, but nothing of its historical background or significance, and if they feel and understand nothing of its emotional content? Indeed, what good is literacy if children, when they are grown, can sing or play music from the printed page, but can't tell the difference between (and perhaps do not like) Bach, Beethoven, Brahms, Stravinsky, or Bartók? Ultimately *knowing* that difference and liking music of many styles begins with children *feeling* the difference and experiencing the many moods and facets of music that are appropriate to their age level — for instance, the difference between songs like *Go Tell Aunt Rhody* and *Deedle Deedle Dumpling, My Son John.*

Enjoying such music begins with being exposed to only the best music in the earliest stages of a child's experience and training. Thus, both the selection of material and its performance are of the greatest importance. If we are to avoid the pitfall of making music literacy (or musical "gymnastics") the end goal, then the selection of proper material is the first consideration. The second is knowing how and when to use the music selected.

How does one know which materials are good and which are not? How does one know which materials are appropriate to the task at hand? For instance: one learns, in studying the Kodály way, that street songs and games are not very good for skill development; they rather should be used for sheer joy in the movement and for socialization. The same is true of many of the most beautiful folk songs — they should be sung for their own sake, for the beauty of the music and the idea the text expresses, not to teach *fa* or *fi*, *ti-ti ta* or form. It follows that basic skills can best be developed through a balanced diet of well-chosen folk music, exercises, and short art examples. The ability to discriminate is becoming more and more difficult, however, now that there is such an explosion and proliferation of possibilities from which to choose. Good choices depend on one's musicianship and on sensitivity to the background and needs of the students being taught.

What *is* musicianship? What is musicality? What are musical "gymnastics"? Can a person be a good musician and not be musical? Can a person be musical and not be a good musician? Can a teacher be successful substituting gymnastics for musicianship and musicality? The answers could provide material for a master's thesis. I will not attempt to discuss possible answers here, but I suggest that these questions are worth thinking about in relation to your own teaching. I would like to comment, however, at the risk of oversimplification, that musicianship is indispensable to every teacher but strangely elusive — sometimes even to the talented; that musicality is sought after by all but too infrequently achieved; that "gymnastics" are highly important in proper perspective but ruinous if overdone.

Musicianship is an all-inclusive term; it is generally assumed that a person who possesses it is versed in all facets of the art of music, yet I have known supposedly good musicians who can read anything at sight, hear internally what they see, write down what they hear, analyze and memorize quickly, who are versed in harmony and counterpoint, know intellectually the literature of a great many periods and styles — yet are unable to communicate a single musical phrase with meaning. How is this possible? I submit that it happens because both students and teachers are too often more concerned with the acquisition of skills for their own sake than with the ultimate purpose of acquiring them.

Let us consider musicianship and musicality for a moment. Is one really different from the other? Interpreting the famous Schumann-based Kodály definition, one might say that musicality is the "heart" of musicianship. The road to musicianship is hard work in all aspects of music — development in basic skills, ear, eye, mind, hand, and heart, and the ability to use those skills to read, sing, play, improvise, and compose (even if only on an elementary level) — also knowledge of literature, history of music, and style.

As to the "heart" part of it, everyone wants to be musical, but *wanting* to be musical is different from *being* it — talking about it is not enough. The musicality of the teacher is of prime importance, and the younger the children you teach, the more important it is, since children learn the most when they are youngest, and since most early learning is basically imitation. The children will imitate you; therefore, you had better be worth imitating!

The way to musicality is complete immersion in the music itself, live music making on any level of which you are capable, and above all, going to concerts, hearing music performed by as many fine artists as possible, and, in the case of music that is already known to you, observing how the performer shapes a phrase, how he or she either exploits or submerges technique in order to communicate the essence of the music. The way is through knowing a great deal of literature and hearing the performances of many artists, through developing a critical sense based on the comparison of both good and bad interpretations, through listening to or, even more important, taking part in performances of a wide variety of music — choral, orchestral, chamber music, opera, and solo.

About musicality, or the "heart" of the music, Kodály said: "I cannot find lessons in the curriculum of any school. And yet, most of the shortcomings are in this area. But it cannot be taught in classes. Psychology might help, and that can be taught, but the rest is supplied by life; the reading of great writers' works, the study of great artists' creations. ... The majority of pupils studying music hardly know anything that is not included in their curriculum, in the strict sense of the term. This is because, as a result of their poor reading abilities, it requires so much time for them to get to know a composition. It is not enough to listen once, fleetingly, to great works: one has to prepare for them and to follow the notes through the pages both before and after hearing them in order to implant them abidingly in one's mind. Personal participation is worth more than anything else." [1] And so, I would say that being a part of last summer's performance of the Mozart Requiem under Péter Erdei's inspired and moving direction did more to increase the musicality of our participants than all the courses they took put together. It is for such experiences that our faculty voted a quite revolutionary step, which will take effect this coming July — namely, to cut out approximately one-fifth of our curriculum by suspending classes one day a week in order to hear and make music with fine artists. Every Thursday, instead of regular classes, we will devote the day to a different period and style of music. Mornings will include an explanation of the music to be heard at that morning's concert; afternoons, students may audit master class performances in cello or voice, play chamber music, or have discussions with the morning's artists; evenings there will be another concert. By such a complete immersion, one can ultimately achieve a sense of security based on knowledge and experience.

I remember so well the first time I dared to play a Mozart concerto in public performance with a group of Boston Symphony musicians, without having taken it to my former teacher for criticism. I remember, in my early twenties, saying to myself, "This is the umpteenth Mozart sonata I have studied. Will I ever be able to learn a Mozart sonata or concerto and know what to do with it, without asking Horszowski first whether I am right or wrong? Will I ever *know* I can interpret the difference between Mozart and Haydn, Beethoven and Schubert, Chopin and Liszt?" The question plagued me so much that I embarked on a project to read through all of the Mozart, Haydn, Beethoven, and Schubert sonatas, the twenty-four Chopin Études, the forty-eight preludes and fugues of Bach's *Well-Tempered Clavier*, the six volumes of Bartók's *Mikrokosmos*, and the works of many other composers — to memorize as much as possible, to attend as many concerts as possible, and to notice the similarities and differences in Beethoven piano sonatas, symphonies, and string quartets — yet I still feel very incomplete because I have not found time to do this in the field of opera.

I remember the tremendous milestone that the performance of Mozart's Concerto K. 271 — learned on my own, without help — represented in my life. As I returned backstage after the final bow, I remember thinking, I have crossed a threshold — I am beginning to be an independent musician; now I *know* I can tell my pupils why they must first sing the melody in the slow movement of a Mozart or Beethoven sonata, before playing it, in order to phrase it musically, why they must detach the bass notes in certain Bach pieces rather than to play them legato, why the ornaments must be played this way and not that, in order for the piece to sound like Bach and not like some other composer. The point I am making is that musicality, or at least a degree of it, *can* be acquired through knowing and experiencing music itself; it is easier if one is born with or has inherited talent, but it can be acquired even by those of very modest or limited ability through study and immersion in the performances of those who have something special to communicate.

The Kodály movement has often been criticized for being too disciplined, too full of drill, too uncreative. Too often this happens because its critics do not see or hear a musical result. To be sure, one of the Kodály system's greatest strengths is in its sequence, its ability to develop sharp, finely honed basic skills in musical literacy. But skills are for a greater purpose and we often get so excited with skills that we forget the end goal. Musical gymnastics are fine if you put them into perspective: they reinforce concepts and develop facility and a feeling of security, but at the expense of musicality they are not worthwhile. Indeed, Kodály often complained that Liszt Academy students played only with their fingers and not with their heads and hearts, just as Anna Russell, that great and talented spoofer of serious music, used to say that "singers have resonance where their brains ought to be."

It is important not to be misunderstood about the relative importance of musicality and literacy. A certain amount of "musical gymnastics" is both necessary and pleasurable for students, whether they are children or adults. Developing one's skills to the point where they are internalized and automatic is a challenge of no small proportions: it is a lifelong pursuit for most, a necessary nuisance for the truly talented (who would rather be making music on a lofty level all of the time), and an exciting new world for those who have never had such skills and suddenly discover they are an obtainable objective.

To be musical, one must select high-quality music for study and performance. To pick good music one must be a good musician. The better a musician you are, the better the music you will pick.

And one cannot be a complete musician without going through a certain amount of musical gymnastics. They *are* important. And so musicianship, musicality, and literacy are inextricably intertwined.

The use of solfege as an effective tool in acquiring literacy and musicianship is beyond argument. No one can deny the importance of acquiring a high degree of facility in solfege, yet I have seen this carried to extremes that amount to a fetish, even in such venerated establishments as the Liszt Academy in Budapest. Some of our own KCA faculty, inspired by the realization that they can, if they work hard enough, do thirty cartwheels a minute blindfolded on a tightrope while simultaneously reciting the alphabet backward in Greek — that is, of course, figuratively speaking — have wanted to accomplish always greater feats in solfege because it challenges them, they *can* do it, they enjoy it, and mastery is its own reward. This is fine, if done in moderation and put into perspective. (I certainly do not want to discourage anyone from attaining as high a degree of solfege ability as possible.) But it must not be substituted for music, and persons who fall into this trap should not delude themselves into thinking that facility in using the elements of music automatically means they possess either good musicianship or musicality.

It is possible, and of course best, to have all of these things — literacy, musicianship, musicality. Without them we can do little, but an overdose or imbalance in any one of these areas will leave both the performer and the listener unsatisfied.

We must guard against being technicians in our teaching, just as performers must realize that the ability to play a thousand notes a minute may make a brilliant but empty performance. Life in today's space-age, computerized, technological society is often spectacular but devoid of meaning. Let us struggle incessantly to find the beautiful and nurture it — for ourselves, in our own teaching and music making first, so that we will have it to give those we teach.

[1] Zoltán Kodály, *Selected Writings* (Budapest: Corvina Press, 1974), p. 198.

25. Teacher Training:
The Ideal and the Real

This chapter is adapted from a paper written for the Sixth International Kodály Society Symposium, Antwerp, Belgium, 1983.

In order to make a distinction between ideal and real conditions of U.S. teacher training in the Kodály approach, the stage on which the Kodály system plays its role needs to be set; that is, there needs to be an understanding of basic conditions in the more traditional approach to music education as the context within which Kodály's ideas must be assimilated.

For the past fifty years or more, one of the major goals of American music education has been music literacy, and in truth, at one time there existed in some parts of the United States a higher standard of music literacy than exists today. Some areas of the Midwest and Northeast even knew a movable-do system and used solfege as a means of teaching sightreading. Some of the old Sacred Harp songbooks found in the South show the use of shaped notes, and a few used hand signals. Texts chosen for songs attempted to teach religious, social, moral, and patriotic values.

In the past fifteen to twenty years the emphasis in traditional music education has changed sharply, and even more so in the past decade. I remember thinking, after returning from a year's study in Hungary in 1967–68, that as soon as American music educators would find there really is a way to bring music literacy to everyone, even the average child, then literacy would cease to be a goal. My reasoning was that if a good way to achieve

short summer courses producing students who know only the "gimmicks" and who are therefore inevitably not successful in the classroom. Most prominent of the other pitfalls stemming from the lack of awareness of Kodály's philosophy are:

1. *Rigidity in interpreting methodology.* For instance, common misconceptions lead teachers to take an uncompromising stand: never use anything but pentatonic songs in early grades, never alter the words of a song, don't use movement (that belongs to Orff!), and above all, don't use Orff instruments.

2. *Mistaking methodology for music.* Often teachers become so fascinated by the fact children *can* learn to read and write music that they press the conscious learning of concepts relentlessly on children who have no previous background in the Kodály system. They abstract and drill elements of rhythm, melody, and form to the exclusion of real music itself and of any sense of joy on the part of the children.

3. *Desire for overnight success.* Many teachers newly exposed to Kodály's ideas, perceiving suddenly the possibility for hitherto undreamed of progress and accomplishment for both themselves and the children they teach, set unrealistic goals, teaching at such a fast pace that no real foundation is laid. Children know hand signals and can tell you the names of rhythm and solfege syllables, but cannot imagine even a *so-mi* interval in their inner hearing, and thus cannot sight-sing even the simplest melodies at sight. Such children do not feel the challenge and reward that comes from good teaching and that results in progress and mastery of skills.

4. *Too short or superficial training.* Most of the problems described above are the result of teachers whose understanding and knowledge of the Kodály concept has been acquired through one- or two-day and one- or two-week workshops, or even mere observation of demonstrations at conferences and conventions. Sometimes their knowledge is limited to reading a book about the Kodály "method." Teachers who have learned in this way usually exhaust all their resources in a

short time and then don't know what to do next, leading to boredom and frustration on the part of their pupils.

5. *Teachers' expectations for their students are too low.* This happens even in the case of teachers well trained in Kodály's concept, and could be termed a general problem in all U.S. education. It is a result of the recent permissive attitude of our society, which allows children to seek and expect great rewards for minimum effort (this is also true of adults in management, in the labor force, and nearly everywhere).

CONCLUSIONS

The above-described problems found in Kodály-inspired teaching are also found in other areas of U.S. music teaching and in general education. They are serious, reflecting trends in the society's overall values and goals, but they need not overwhelm us or cause us to despair. The ideal condition, as projected in the early part of this paper, is something we haven't yet reached and probably never will reach. Nevertheless, we have made substantial progress and must not allow ourselves to become discouraged along the way because many facets of our society seem to run counter to the conditions that produced the ideal result in Hungary, or because obstacles are put in our way. We need to keep our minds on the ideal and to keep struggling for improvement, for the truth is that Kodály's ideas have given us a vision and a hope that we have only rarely glimpsed until now — namely, that it may at last be possible, with a beautifully implemented Kodály program, to cultivate those regions of the human soul that Kodály has so often said could be illuminated only by music.

In closing, let me leave with you the words of another great humanist philosopher, Dag Hammarskjöld: "Never measure the height of a mountain till you have reached the top; then you will see how low it was." [1] Many of us will never reach the top; others will reach it only to find, as Hammarskjöld says, that it was, in reality, too low, and that they must start the ascent all over again of a higher peak. Kodály loved mountains — they are often dangerous, sometimes impregnable, unconquerable, inaccessible, but oh, so beautiful! May our future efforts lead us all to mountaintop experiences.

[1] Dag Hammerskjöld, *Markings* (New York: Knopf, 1965), p. 7.

26. The Importance of Kodály Training for Performers

This chapter is adapted from a paper read at the 1986 Organization of American Kodály Educators Conference, St. Louis, Missouri, and at the Eighth International Kodály Society Symposium, Kecskemét, Hungary, August 6, 1987.

Kodály complained in the 1950s that students being graduated from the Liszt Academy could play a thousand notes a minute but had no message, no interpretive powers. Sir Yehudi Menuhin had a prodigious technique as a child, but didn't really know what he was playing. As he grew older, he was so unable to memorize and fearful of breakdown on the stage that he had to withdraw from the concert stage for a period of years and begin all over again to understand and learn the structure of music.

I remember Ruth Slencynska, a quite incredible child prodigy who astounded everyone with her dazzling technique. Her father, who made millions of dollars from her performances, made her practice most of the day and night, practically chaining her to a piano; ultimately she rebelled and refused to have anything to do with music for years. When she returned to the concert stage as a young adult, critics were harsh on her and it was said that her playing was hard, tense, and without feeling, that she probably had little to express, having had too limited experience or contact with real life when growing up. One of her students who came to us for Kodály training described her as an embittered teacher and a slave driver.

Irving Berlin, a composer of some of America's most beautiful and beloved popular songs, is purported to have been able to play only in the key of

— not abruptly or dramatically, but slowly and consistently. People who hear me now say that I play much better than twenty years ago, yet I never practice (simply because I never have time).

The subject of musical influences on a performer is a fascinating one. I would like to describe for you what I was like as a very young performer, my subsequent influences, and the latest transformation wrought by my coming into contact with the Kodály concept. My early training was inconsequential, or rather I should say, the consequences of it were nil. At the age of eighteen I had no technique, had never played a scale in my life, couldn't read anything at sight — I was still in the deciphering stage when I learned new pieces. Unless I had at least a one-day warning, a call to substitute for the head of music, who played hymns for chapel in the small liberal arts college I was then attending, was enough to throw me into a state of complete panic. I would simply forgo all my homework and practice for two hours that night or until I had memorized the hymn. One of the difficulties with my early instruction was that no one realized I had talent, and I myself didn't think it was unusual that I could play most anything I heard by ear. At fourteen I didn't know what absolute pitch was and thought that anyone who played the piano could do that too.

When I was eighteen my piano teacher could no longer cope with me and turned me over to Helen Hopekirk, a wonderful eighty-five-year-old Scottish concert pianist, also a composer, who had settled in the United States and become the terror of the New England Conservatory piano faculty. A student of Leschetizky, she was a friend and contemporary of Paderewski and had premiered Tchaikovsky's Piano Concerto No. 1 in Glasgow before coming to America. This remarkable lady terrified me but made me musical. She discovered that I couldn't read, but didn't care so long as I played musically. I was very shy and quite inhibited at eighteen; feeling my tenseness and woodenness, she ordered me to take the chair I was sitting on at the piano and dance with it for a partner, while she played the Gavotte from Bach's Fifth French Suite! She felt I had no rhythm. I can still feel the embarrassment of my struggle with that horrid chair, but I got the point. Rather than suffer such an indignity again, I became loose as a goose at my next lesson and have had a special feeling for gavottes ever since!

I did not know until several years later, after I had become acquainted with the Kodály concept, that Helen Hopekirk was having the same ideas about folk music, composition, and culture in Scotland that Kodály had had at just about the same time in Hungary. I discovered this only recently when rereading the preface she had written to a book of Hebridean folk songs she had collected and arranged for solo voices with art song–style accompaniments. Helen Hopekirk was a pianist of the Romantic tradition whose heart and style, rooted in the late nineteenth century, found their way into both my technique and my sense of style.

My next musical influence shall remain nameless, as he became a famous American musical personality. Truly a remarkable musician, he was obsessed with technique but had little soul. I will not dwell on this experience except to say that I shall always be grateful to him, since I learned a great deal about what not to do in both technical and musical matters.

I then fell miraculously, through an audition for Rudolf Serkin, into the hands of one of the most wonderful teachers of this century — Mieczyslaw Horszowski. Now ninety-five years old, he is almost totally blind, but still performs and teaches at the Curtis Institute of Music in Philadelphia.† Many of today's famous performers were students of his, and he is revered by the great for his scholarship, simplicity, humility, and integrity. A man smaller in stature than Artur Rubinstein, Horszowski is nevertheless a giant. He speaks ten languages, was referred to in his youth as another Mozart, and knows as much about art, literature, and science as about music. At my very first lesson, after I had finished playing the first movement of Beethoven's Third Piano Concerto, he asked me to read the slow movement at sight, and thereby discovered, to his obvious dismay, that I couldn't read music. Here I was — twenty-four years old, had

†Horszowski celebrated his hundredth birthday in June 1992 and is still teaching at Curtis.

played twice with the Boston Pops Orchestra, given many solo recitals, but was still in the deciphering stage.

Horszowski taught me style and scholarship. I constantly begged him to help me technically, but he always said that the technique must come from the music. "You must know how you want the music to sound and what you want to say — only then will you find the means to say it. If you want to play it a certain way badly enough, you will find the technical means to do it." How little I understood what he really meant.

I struggled and struggled by myself to overcome my technical deficiencies. I practiced scales, arpeggios, trills, and octaves, but my technique improved little. Even worse, my rhythm was unstable because of the uncertainty of my technique. And the worst nightmare of all was my nerves in performance. I hated performing, because I never played in public as well as I knew I could or should. I had set a standard for myself but was not reaching it. I performed because my mother had set her heart on my being a concert pianist; I didn't want to hurt her, but my heart was not in it. Yet the odd thing was that in my own living room with a group of friends, I felt the need and the ability to communicate; in this setting I loved to play (and still do).

Although I finally did improve my reading ability quite dramatically, through a book Horszowski gave me by Paul Hindemith called *Elementary Training for Musicians*, I was still uncomfortable as a performer. Meanwhile, I had to support myself through teaching. In the 1940s it was still enough to have a soloist diploma, which I had acquired from the Longy School of Music in Cambridge, Massachusetts, and to have studied with a man of Horszowski's stature. People began to be very degree conscious in the musical field in the 1950s, and so I went to New England Conservatory, graduating with a Bachelor of Music degree in piano performance and two years later with a Master of Music degree in chamber music. The instruction in piano I received there could not compare with Horszowski's, and time more or less stood still for me, though at that time I developed a serious interest in composition and in contemporary music, especially Bartók's music.

Following my mother's death in 1957, I felt relieved of the necessity of performing in public and have done little of it since. I kept on playing, however, because I could not stay away from the piano. Over the years I taught many gifted piano students, most of whom could not read music either. I concluded that something must be wrong with their foundation and early training.

When I first heard of the Kodály concept, it occurred to me that here might be an answer to my students' literacy problems. After only a few weeks of study in Hungary, it quickly became clear that the way Hungarian children were learning music in school was almost exactly the way I was trying to teach my individual piano students — namely, I was always trying to get them to learn everything consciously and automatically as a skill they could depend upon, so that they could pick up a piece of music and learn it for their own pleasure. The biggest problem was that this process took forever; when a student had only one or two forty-five-minute lessons weekly, it left no time for the technical problems of the instrument or the music itself. Yet in Hungary, children had acquired the basic language of music by third or fourth grade, usually even before they started to learn an instrument!

The 1967–68 year of study revolutionized my piano teaching; it also resulted in my deciding to teach three-year-olds instead of high school and college students. What I didn't realize until some time after I returned home was what effect all that training and observation had had on my own personal musicianship and attitude toward performance.

Though I had never had any problem with either ear training or dictation because of my absolute pitch, I found that I was now hearing, in symphonic works I had known for years, all kinds of inner parts I had never discovered before. I found all sorts of melodic fragments in Bach's fugues I had never considered important before. And wonder of wonders, I could now read in seven clefs! This meant I no longer had to worry about transposing instruments in conducting the community orchestra I had started some years before at Dana Hall — all I had to do now was substitute another clef to hear the score at concert pitch.

"Communication and the Kodály Concept." Hunter Art Museum, Chattanooga, Tennessee, January 1978.

"Report to Canada." Canadian Kodály Conference, Vancouver, British Columbia, 1978.

"Hungary Will Never Outgrow Kodály." Rebuttal to article "Has Hungary Outgrown Kodály?" *Music Educators Journal,* February 1978.

"The Impact of the Kodály Philosophy on American Education." NAIS Conference, New York City, March 1978.

"KCA: Young and New, Old and Established." Graduation Address, First KCA Summer Course, 1978.

* "Survival for Innovative Trends in Music Education." KCA Day, 1979.

* "Kodály Training: Musicality or Gymnastics?" OAKE Conference, Bloomington, Indiana, March 1980.

"Eclectic Music Education: Homogenized Excellence or Mediocrity?" MENC National Conference, Miami, Florida, April 1980.

"The Goal of a Perceptive Listener." MENC National Conference, Miami, Florida, April 1980.

"Controlling Destiny: The Individual's Role." Opening Address, KCA Summer Course, 1980.

* "Kodály in Context of the Eighties." KCA Day, March 1981; *Midwest Kodály Educators Bulletin,* July 1982 (here retitled "Kodály in the 1980s").

* "Kodály and the Quality of Life." KCA fund-raising dinner, Chicago, Illinois, May 1981.

"The Strength of Kodály's Philosophy." Graduation Address, KCA Summer Course, 1981.

"Kodály Music for Learning-Disabled Children." Fifth International Kodály Symposium, Sapporo, Japan, August 1981; Second International MEH Symposium, Provo, Utah, August 1981.

* "Kodály Values for a Society in Crisis." Opening Address, KCA Summer Course, 1982.

* "The Adaptation of Kodály's Concept of Music Education in America: Early Steps — An Historical Perspective." Tenth International Kodály Seminar, Kecskemét, Hungary, July 1982. *IKS Bulletin,* 1983 (here retitled "Adapting the Kodály Concept in America, 1965–1982").

* "Hold Fast to Dreams." Graduation Address, KCA Summer Course, 1982.

[237]

"Where Do We Go from Here?" Opening Address, KCA Academic Year, September 1982.

"Reflections on Zoltán Kodály's Centennial." Kodály Centennial, Boston University, November 1982.

"Report on the Kodály Movement in America." International Centennial Conference of the Hungarian Kodály Society, Budapest, December 1982.

* "Kodály for Large Cities: The Boston Experience." MENC Eastern Division Convention, February 1983. *Massachusetts Music Educators News* 32, no. 3 (1984).

* "Kodály's Message: Unsuspected Gold." OAKE Conference, Seattle, Washington, March 1983.

* "Music for Our Time." Opening Address, KCA Summer Course, 1983 (here retitled "The Gulf Between Performers and Educators").

"The Joy of Giving." Graduation Address, KCA Summer Course, 1983.

* "Teacher Training: The Ideal and the Real." For Sixth IKS Symposium, Antwerp, Belgium, 1983.

"Preserving Excellence." Graduation Address, KCA Summer Course, 1984.

"The Risk Takers." Opening Address, KCA Academic Year, September 1984.

* "The Practicality and Adaptability of Kodály's Philosophy." Maine Music Educators Conference, May 1985.

* "The Adaptation of Kodály's Ideas to Another Culture." For Seventh IKS Symposium, London, England, July 1985.

"Using the Kodály Approach with Emotionally Disturbed Children." Fourth International MEH Symposium, Goldwater Memorial Hospital, New York, N.Y., August 1985.

"The Kodály Concept: In Service of Others." Opening Address, KCA Academic Year, 1985.

* "The Importance of Kodály Training for Performers." OAKE Conference, St. Louis, Missouri, 1986; Eighth IKS Symposium, Kecskemét, Hungary, August 1987.

"A Little Bit of History and a New Opportunity." Opening Address, Summer Course, Kecskemét, Hungary, July 1986.

"A New Dimension." Closing Exercises, Summer Course, Kecskemét, Hungary, August 1986.

* "KCA in Context of the Worldwide Movement: The First Ten Years — The Future." Opening Address, KCA Summer Course, July 1987 (here retitled "KCA and the Worldwide Kodály Movement").

* "And Miles to Go Before I Sleep." Graduation Address, KCA Summer Course, 1987.

* "The Human Value of the Kodály Approach." Opening Address, KCA Summer Session, July 1988.

* "What Is Kodály Training?" KCA Open House, November 1988.

* "An End and a Beginning." Closing Address, Summer Course, Kecskemét, Hungary, August 1989.

* "An Historical Perspective and a Look at the Future." Dana School of Music, KCA Fifteenth Anniversary, April 11, 1992.

* "Bridging the Gap: Kodály the Educator and Kodály the Composer." *KCA Newsletter*, June 1992.

"What's in a Name?" *KCA Newsletter*, June 1992.

"The High Cost of Quality Materials." *KCA Newsletter*, May 1993.

Chronology

1940	Denise Bacon graduates from Music Course of Pine Manor Junior College. Joins music faculty of Dana Hall School, Wellesley, Massachusetts; head of Dana Hall Music Department 1948–69.
1942–62	Limited concert career combined with teaching.
1943	Graduates from Longy School of Music with Soloist Diploma.
1957	Founds Dana School of Music for the Wellesley community.
1964	First summer workshop in Orff method, Dana School of Music.
1965	Attends Mary Helen Richards's workshop, Syracuse, New York. First meeting with Kodály, Dartmouth College, Hanover, New Hampshire.
1966	Subsequent meetings with Kodály, at Stanford University, Palo Alto, California, and ISME Conference, Interlochen, Michigan.
1967	Receives Braitmayer Foundation and Dana Hall trustee grants for sabbatical year of study in Hungary and Salzburg.
1968	Brings Péter Erdei to the United States from Hungary. First experiments in Winchester, Massachusetts, public schools.
1969	July: Workshop at Dana School of Music with leading teachers from Orff Institute in Salzburg and Kodály master teachers from Hungary.
	August: Notification of Ford Foundation grant to establish institute for training of teachers in Kodály concept.

1969   September: Establishment of the Kodály Musical Training Institute (KMTI).

October: Mrs. Kodály and Márta Nemesszeghy visit KMTI to make long-range plans with Péter Erdei and Denise Bacon and devise specific academic program. First academic class: Toni Locke, Keith Knighton, Lee Robbins, Jane Thurber.

1970   Katalin Komlós arrives to develop KMTI folk song collection. Pilot class trip to Hungary to make the film *Let's Sing Together* with Hungarian children.

Klára Kokas arrives to develop research program.

First KMTI summer course held at the Kecskemét Singing Primary School, Kecskemét, Hungary, in conjunction with First International Kodály Seminar.

First KMTI academic-year class goes to Hungary to complete second year of Diploma Course program at Liszt Academy, Budapest.

1971   Six-year agreement with Needham, Massachusetts, public schools for two model school Kodály programs, one daily, one twice weekly.

First inner-city Boston model school program, Taft School, Brighton.

Establishment of West Hartford pilot project.

First KMTI Kodály-emphasis master's degree established with New England Conservatory.

First KMTI summer course in the United States, University of Bridgeport, Connecticut.

First Diploma Course graduates (1969 class).

First KMTI publication: *Let's Sing Together for 3-, 4-, and 5-Year-Olds*, Boosey and Hawkes.

1972   Establishment of KMTI one-year certificate course (in the United States only).

1973   Publication of *46 Two-Part American Folk Songs for Elementary Grades*, KMTI (subsequent editions by KCA).

Publication of *Kodály for Beginning Levels*, KMTI.

College Conference of twelve institutions at third

KMTI summer course (Wellesley College) to establish master's degree Kodály-emphasis programs.

1974	Publication of 150 *American Folk Songs to Sing, Read and Play,* Boosey and Hawkes.
	Extension Division initiated.
1975	Zoltán Kodály Pedagogical Institute of Music in Kecskemét, Hungary, opens.
	Kodály Research Seminar with Klára Kokas, KMTI summer course at Wellesley College.
	Pilot Kodály program established at Community School 61, South Bronx, New York City, through Exxon grant.
	First teacher-training course in college-level theory with Erzsébet Hegyi, Wellesley College.
1976–78	Research project on learning-disabled children.
1976–79	Teacher-Training Curriculum Project, Happy Valley School, Peterborough, New Hampshire.
1976–79	Non-Musical Effects of Kodály Musical Training Research Project.
1977	Establishment of the Kodály Center of America, West Newton, Massachusetts.
	Publication of 50 *Easy Two-Part Exercises,* Schott (now European American).
1978	Publication of 185 *Easy Unison Pentatonic Exercises,* KCA.
	First KCA summer course, Southeastern Massachusetts University, North Dartmouth, Massachusetts. (Subsequent SMU courses annually, 1979 through 1985.)
1980	Establishment of Kodály program in Chattanooga and Hamilton County, Tennessee, public schools, through Lyndhurst Foundation and Chattanooga Education in Musical Arts Association.
1981	Second research project on learning-disabled children.
1982	KCA celebrations of Kodály Centennial in Boston and Chicago.
1983	KCA moves to 295 Adams Street, Newton, Massachusetts.

1985	Cambridge Community Center program initiated.
1986	First KCA four-week summer course at the Kecskemét Institute, Hungary.
1987–88	KCA summer courses at Great Woods, Norton, Massachusetts.
1989	KCA summer course in Kecskemét in conjunction with the fifteenth international Kodály seminar.
1990	KCA moves to 15 Denton Road, Wellesley, Massachusetts.
	KCA summer course transferred to Capital University, Columbus, Ohio.
1991	KCA merges teacher-training program with Capital's Kodály program.
1992	KCA Fifteenth Anniversary Celebration, April 11.
	KMTI joins KCA at Capital University for summer course.
	Publication of *Ta And Ti Bones* by Keith Knighton, KCA.
1993	Capital, KCA, and KMTI Kodály programs merge to become the Kodály Center at Capital University, with KCA continuing for the immediate future as an independent resource center.

Index